HEALING
with
GEMSTONES

HEALING
with
GEMSTONES

Pamela Louise Chase
and
Jonathan Pawlik

NEW PAGE BOOKS
A division of The Career Press, Inc.
Franklin Lakes, NJ

HEALING WITH GEMSTONES
Typeset by Stacey A. Farkas
Cover design by Cheryl Cohan Finbow
Printed in the U.S.A. by Book-mart Press

To order this title, please call toll-free 1-800-CAREER-1 (NJ and Canada: 201-848-0310) to order using VISA or MasterCard, or for further information on books from Career Press.

The Career Press, Inc., 3 Tice Road, PO Box 687,
Franklin Lakes, NJ 07417
www.careerpress.com
www.newpagebooks.com

Library of Congress Cataloging-in-Publication Data

Chase, Pamela.
    Healing with gemstones / by Pamela Louise Chase and Jonathan Pawlik.
        p. cm.
    Rev. ed. of: The Newcastle guide to healing with gemstones.
    Includes bibliographical references and index.
    ISBN 1-56414-547-6
    1. Precious stones—Psychic aspects. I. Pawlik, Jonathan. II Chase, Pamela. Newcastle guide to healing with gemstones.

BF1442.P74 C47 2002
133'.25538—dc21

                                                    2001044361

Disclaimer

This book is not intended to diagnose, prescribe, or treat any ailment, nor is it intended in any way as a replacement for medical consultation when needed. The author and publisher of this book do not guarantee the efficacy of any of the methods herein described, and strongly suggest that, at the first suspicion of any disease or disorder, the reader consult a physician.

Acknowledgments

We extend our thanks to the Devas for their love and support, which is the foundation of this book and of our lives.

We also wish to thank Robert Brink, our editor, for his care and attention to details; and the people at New Page Books for their role in sharing these words with you.

CONTENTS

Preface   17

Part 1: Exploring the World of Gemstones   19

Chapter 1. Physical Aspects of Gemstones   21

Definitions 21
The Crystal or the Gemstone Path? 22
Hardness 22
Chemical Composition 23
Crystalline Structure 23
Color 25
Other Properties Used to Identify Gemstones 27
Cutting and Polishing 28
Gem Substitutes 28
Types of Deposits and Mining 29
Mineral Families 30

Chapter 2. Spiritual Aspects of Gemstones   33

Reviewing Life-force Energy and 34
the Human Energy System

The Spiritual Reality of the Devic 37
Kingdoms of Nature

The Influence of Beliefs upon Our Perceptions 41
of Gemstone Qualities

Gemstone Correlations: Astrology and 42
Other Metaphysical Belief Systems

Choosing Gemstones 43

Caring for Gemstones 44

Asking for Intuitive Guidance 46

How to Use a Crystal Pendulum 47

Saturation 51

Chapter 3. Learning About Gem Energy: 53
Color, Sound, and Chakra Affinities

Perspective 1: Color 54

Perspective 2: Sound... 58

Perspective 3: Chakra and the Subtle Body Affinities 61

Chapter 4. Learning About Gem Energy: 67
The Healing Process & the 4 Elements

Perspective 4: Healing with the 3-step Process 67

Perspective 5: The 4 Elements of Nature 72

Part 2: The Individual Gemstones   75

Chapter 5. Individual Gemstones and   77
Metallic Elements

The Gemstones

Alexanderite 77

Amazonite 79

Amber 81

Amethyst 82

Apatite 83

Aquamarine 85

Aventurine 86

Azurite 88

Bloodstone 89

Blue Lace Agate 90

Calcite 92

Carnelian 94

Celestite 96

Chalcedony 98

Charoite 99

Chrysocolla 100

Chrysoprase 102

Citrine 103

Coral 104

Diamond 107

Dioptase 109

Emerald 110

Fire Agate 111

Fluorite 113

Galena 115

Garnet 117

Gem Silica 118

Heliodor 119

Hematite 121

Iolite 122

Jade 124

Jasper 125

Jet 126

Kunzite 128

Kyanite 130

Labradorite 131

Lapis Lazuli 133

Larimar 135

Lepidolite 137

Magnetite 138

Malachite 139

Moldavite 140

Moonstone 143

Moss Agate 144

Obsidian 145

Opal 147

Pearl 149

Peridot 151

Pyrite 152

Rhodochrosite 153

Rhodonite 155

Rose Quartz 156

Ruby 157

Rutilated Quartz 158

Sapphire 160

Selenite 162

Smoky Quartz 163

Sodalite 164

Spinel (Red) 166

Sugilite 167

Sunstone (Orange) 168

Tiger's Eye 170

Topaz 171

Tourmaline 174

Turquoise 180

Ulexite 181

Vanadinite 183

Yellow Orthoclase Feldspar (Yellow Sunstone) 184

Zircon 186

The Metals

Copper 187

Gold 189

Silver 190

Part 3: Cocreating with Gemstones   193
    for Healing

Chapter 6. Gem Essences: 195
    Their Use and Preparation

Water As a Medium for Transfer 196

The Mechanical Method of Making Gem Essences 197

The Consciousness Method of Making Gem Essences 199

Taking the Gem Essences 201

Gem Essence for Clients 211

Chapter 7. Gemstones and Healing   221

The Thymus Gland 222

3 Criteria for Layouts 224

Working with 1 or 2 Stones..225

Choosing and Working with a Layout 226

Gemstones and Clear Quartz Crystal........................ 227

Conclusion 232

Chapter 8. Planetary Overview   233

The Overlighting Deva of the Mineral Kingdom 233

The Overlighting Deva for Planet Earth 236

Endnotes   239

Bibliography   241

Index   243

About the Authors   255

List of Charts and Illustrations

Figure 1-1. The Mohs' Scale of Hardness 23

Figure 1-2. The Cubic System 24

Figure 1-3. The Hexagonal System 24

Figure 1-4. The Tetragonal System 24

Figure 1-5. The Orthorhombic System 24

Figure 1-6. The Monoclinic System 25

Figure 1-7. The Triclinic System 25

Figure 1-8. The Trigonal System 25

Figure 2-1. Pendulum Arc for Specific Qualities 50

Figure 3-1. Diagram of the Chakras and the Thymus Gland 64

Figure 3-2. Summary of Chakra Information 65

Figure 4-1. The Frequency Band 71

Figure 6-1. How Often and How Much Essence 203

Figure 6-2. Percentage Correlation for Essences 204

Figure 6-3. Clearing—Root Through Throat 205

Figure 6-4. Clearing—Third Eye and Crown 206

Figure 6-5. Building and Spiritual Expansion—Root 207
and Lower Abdomen

Figure 6-6. Building and Spiritual Expansion—Solar Plexus 208

Figure 6-7. Building and Spiritual Expansion—Heart 209
and Throat

Figure 6-8. Building and Spiritual Expansion—Third Eye 210
and Crown

Figure 6-9. Gemstone Affiliations and Soul Tones 213

Figure 7-1. Clockwise Infusion 226

Figure 7-2. 3-Crystal Grid-Infusing 227

Figure 7-3. 3-Crystal Grid-Y 227

Figure 7-4. Gemstone Chakra Affinities for Clearing 229

Figure 7-5. Gemstone Chakra Affinities for Building and 230
Spiritual Expansion

PREFACE

Anyone who has had a pet knows the pure trust and love that an animal so freely shares. We often take this love for granted, not fully understanding how we are being served in this way. Nevertheless, we have been loved, healed, and cheered on by the devotion of our pets. It is time for us to understand that all living things have a Consciousness that gives and receives compassion, and that we are intimately connected with the Kingdoms of Nature through our mutual service to each other. Our aim in this book is to help you deepen your connection with Nature. Although this perspective is quite different from the way we as a culture currently perceive Nature, it is more in tune with the wisdom of the Native Americans. We also hope that you will learn to see stones as friends and guides rather than as inanimate objects to be taken for granted. When we admire the beauty in all things, including stones, we are also affirming Nature.

This book has been written to share the spiritual healing gifts of the Mineral Kingdom with those of you who are working on a daily basis with personal growth. When we began work on this book, we originally thought that we would be involved in many different kinds of activities. Our plans "fell through," however, and instead, we were sent in solitude to clean and beautify the houses of our own minds. It seemed like just when I would get one dusty room of personal doubts tidied up, the dust would collect somewhere else. The purpose of this book is to aid you in the daily discipline of "housecleaning" your thoughts, and it includes affirmations, as well as many other ways, to incorporate gemstones to this end.

Jonathan and I turned to Nature, as we do when we are in solitude, and we opened ourselves to the healing of the stones. It took the intensity of solitude to learn what we needed to learn, and to write about it. Working with the stones was a journey of the Soul, and like the journey of the tarot Fool, we learned the lessons of many lifetimes. Our personal journey was filled with joy and a sense that all was unfolding according to plan.

The material in the text in *this typeface* has been channeled through Jonathan by different Devas, which we consider to be the Higher Selves of the Kingdoms of Nature. We hope that you will also sense the joy and compassion of the Mineral Kingdom as you read, and find your own personal relationship with the stones.

—Pamela Louise Chase

Part 1

EXPLORING THE WORLD OF GEMSTONES

I n the four chapters of Part 1, we share some of the practices that helped develop our skills in understanding the qualities of gemstones. These practices take patience and are not learned overnight, but they are enjoyable and will help expand your intuitive understanding in other areas. Chapter 1 is an introduction to the physical qualities by which gemstones are identified. We have pondered over the possible parallels between the physical and spiritual qualities of gemstones, and we leave you to explore this issue. Chapter 2 deals with the spiritual aspects of gemstones and acquaints us with the unifying concept of life force energy and the human energy system. We introduce the Devas and discuss the central role of our personal beliefs in Spiritual perception and understanding of the Higher Realms. Finally, we review some basics of choosing and caring for gemstones. Chapter 3 describes three of the five perspectives from which we have learned about gemstones: color, sound, and chakra and subtle body affinities. Chapter 4 discusses two final perspectives on learning about gem energy: the three-step process of healing and the four elements of Nature. These five perspectives are the routes we took in developing our intuitive discrimination. We have detailed them in the hope that your own process may be made easier.

Chapter 1

PHYSICAL ASPECTS
OF GEMSTONES

Definitions

I n this chapter we will get acquainted with gemstones by taking a look at how gemologists study and identify their physical properties. We will begin by defining some terms. A *mineral* is a naturally occurring inorganic solid having a definite chemical composition and an internal structure that is geometrically uniform. Most of the stones that we will talk about in this book are *minerals,* except for amber, coral, and pearl, which are organic in origin. The term *rock* generally refers to aggregates of minerals that have not been tampered with by humans. A *gemstone* is a mineral with certain physical properties that are valued by the jewelry trade, such as hardness, durability, and brilliance when cut. The term *crystal* is commonly used in referring to gemstones because of the geometrical symmetry of their internal structure. We will use the term *crystal* to specifically refer to clear quartz crystals. Finally, the word *stone* collectively refers to minerals, gemstones, or rocks. We will use these terms interchangeably, and the stones we have chosen are readily available, relatively inexpensive in their rough form, and ones that we have personally found to be beneficial.

The Crystal or the Gemstone Path?

When you are beginning to work with the Mineral Kingdom, it can be helpful to develop your sensitivity with one mineral. Broadening your knowledge of other stones will then be easier. Clear quartz crystal can be a good stone to begin with for this purpose. Its balanced structure and piezoelectric properties contribute to its qualities of versatility and amplification of intuitive communication skills. We consider it to be a "master teacher" of the Mineral Kingdom.

However, it is also possible to begin work with a gemstone to which you feel attracted, using this book as a guide. Gemstones, because of their colors, are more specific in the range of their functions. Getting to know the gemstones is like meeting individual personalities, and helps to enrich your life through a wider experience of the Mineral Kingdom. If you are attracted to stones as a tool for spiritual growth, you will probably be eager to become acquainted with both clear quartz and other gemstones as well. This book is devoted to describing a number of gemstones and ways in which you can work with clear quartz crystal to amplify your knowledge of other stones.

Hardness

There are a number of distinguishing characteristics that are used in identifying a gemstone. The first is *hardness,* its resistance to abrasion or scratching. A Viennese mineralogist named Friedrich Mohs (1773–1839), developed the most common scale by defining scratch hardness as the resistance of a mineral when scratched with a pointed testing object. Figure 1-1 includes 10 minerals that are listed in their order of hardness on the Mohs' scale from 1 to 10, along with the Mohs' values of common items such as a fingernail and a copper coin.

By this scale a stone that remains unmarred after being scratched by a piece of window glass would have a hardness of more than 5 1/2. In general, jewelry is made from gemstones that test 7 or harder, because the softer minerals scratch more easily and are not as durable. Currently, the scratch hardness test has been largely abandoned in favor of optical testing methods for identifying gemstones. However, this test can still be useful if you simply want to know something about a rock that you pick up off the ground.

Figure 1-1. The Mohs' Scale of Hardness		
1. talc		6. feldspar
2. gypsum	(fingernail 2 1/2)	7. quartz
3. calcite	(copper coin 3)	8. topaz
4. fluorite		9. corundum
5. apatite	(window glass 5 1/2)	10. diamond

Chemical Composition

Minerals can also be identified chemically. Most of the better known gems are mineral oxides or silicates. For example, all members of the quartz family, including clear quartz crystal, amethyst, and rose quartz, are silicon dioxide (SiO_2). Ruby and sapphire are aluminum oxide (Al_2O_3), and emerald, aquamarine, and beryl are aluminum beryllium silicate ($Al_2Be_3(Si_6O_{18})$). Oxides and silicates are often stable enough in their composition to resist decomposition, unlike sulphides and other mineral groupings. However, minerals with the same chemical composition can be quite different. Graphite and diamond are both carbon, but they are at opposite ends of the hardness scale because their crystalline structure is very different.

Crystalline Structure

Gemstones are highly structured, orderly lattices of molecules. The outer planes and surfaces of a stone can reflect the geometry of the internal structure. Most gemstones are not regularly shaped because some crystal faces are more pronounced, but the angle between the faces remains constant. Gemstones are classified into seven categories of crystalline structures, with varying degrees of symmetry. The explanation of the categories in Figures 1-2 through 1-8 comes from *The Spiritual Value of Gemstones* by Wallace G. Richardson and Lenora Huett.[1]

Note: The diagrams below will give a better visual presentation of the various basic crystal formations.

FIGURE 1-2. *The cubic system,* with three equal axes (a_1, a_2, a_3), arranged normal to each other:

FIGURE 1-3. *The hexagonal system,* with four axes, three of which are arranged in one plane at 120° angles to each other. The main axis (c-axis) is normal to these three; it is an axis of sixfold symmetry:

FIGURE 1-4. *The tetragonal system,* having two equal axes at 90° to each other (a_1 and a_2), and normal to these the main axis with fourfold symmetry:

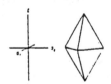

FIGURE 1-5. *The orthorhombic system,* with three unique axes (a, b, and c) at 90° to each other:

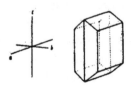

Physical Aspects of Gemstones

Figure 1-6.- *The monoclinic system,* having three unequal axes (a, b, and c) at an obtuse angle to each other; b is normal to the plane formed by a and c:

Figure 1-7. *The triclinic system,* having three axes of unequal length (a, b and c), all at obtuse angles to each other:

Figure 1-8. *The trigonal system,* using the same pattern as the hexogonal system. The main axis, however, has threefold symmetry only. This system is sometimes called the rhombohedral:

Color

One of the most fascinating aspects of gemstones is the way in which they absorb and reflect light. When light passes through a gemstone with no interruption, it is *transparent,* like clear quartz crystal. If a certain wavelength of light is absorbed, the remaining mixture produces a color, and the gemstone is *translucent* or *opaque. Translucent* means allowing the passage of light, but not primarily a clear view of any object. Moonstone and carnelian are examples of translucent stones. *Opaque* stones, such as blue lace agate and lapis lazuli, are impervious to light. If all the light is absorbed, then the stone appears black, as in black tourmaline. If all the wavelengths are absorbed in the same degree, the stone is a dull white or gray, as in white chalcedony.

Many gemstones, such as members of the quartz family, vary widely in color because of very small amounts of dispersed *impurities.* Clear quartz crystal becomes the deep violet of amethyst due to minute traces of iron. Rose quartz gets its pink color from manganese or titanium. Other stones, such as peridot and garnet, are naturally colored without impurities.

Holes, bubbles, and irregularities in the crystalline structure are classified as *inclusions.* Inclusions can change the color, optical properties, and mechanical resistance of a stone, and can also give certain stones their unique qualities. The play of colors in labradorite and opal are due to inclusions. During the formation of a corundum crystal, needle-like inclusions of rutile can form a hexagonal pattern, which gives the effect of a six-rayed star in a cut stone. Such stones are known as star sapphires and star rubies.

The internal structures of a gemstone can act as a filter permitting certain kinds of light to pass through. Some gems will transmit different colors depending on the direction in which light passes through the stone. This phenomenon is called *pleochroism,* of which kunzite is an example. Kunzite can look lavender or pink, depending on which way you hold it to the light.

Other effects can also alter color. Clear quartz, which has been exposed to radioactivity found at great underground depths, absorbs ultraviolet light and becomes smoky quartz. Amethyst, rose quartz, and kunzite can become paler when exposed to direct sunlight over a period of time.

Some stones are heat-treated to change their colors. For example, amethyst is heated several hundred degrees to become reddish yellow citrine. In fact, many citrines are heat-treated amethyst. Other examples include dark green tourmalines heated to produce a lighter green. Practically all the deep blue aquamarine that is commonly available is heat-treated green or yellow beryl. Dealers are not required by law to state whether or not their stones have been heat-treated.

The color of a gem is further described according to its hue, tint, and intensity. Throughout history, the most popular stones have been those with hues of red, green, or blue; dark rather than light tints; and high intensity. The darkest colored stones are cut thicker so that their color deepens.

Other Properties Used to Identify Gemstones

There are several other properties used to identify gemstones. The first is *cleavage,* a term used to describe how gems split along certain flat planes. This property is related to their atomic structure. Stone setters must take the stone's cleavage into account, because if the stone is tapped too strongly or given too much pressure, it will split along cleavage lines. Minerals that break easily are said to have perfect cleavage, and faceted gemstones with perfect cleavage indicate an artist's skill in handling them. Quartz does not break evenly or cleanly in any direction. In other words, it does not cleave. This lack of cleavage is a clue in identifying quartz. Some minerals such as calcite will cleave equally well in three directions, whereas topaz cleaves perfectly in only one direction. It is possible to see the cleavage planes by holding the stone and turning it slowly in the light. When the angle is right, you can see the reflection of light from many small parallel and lustrous surfaces, which are scattered at different levels along the break.

Another property is the *refractive index.* When you place a stick in water at a slant, the stick looks broken at the water level. This phenomenon is caused by the refraction of light as it leaves the air and enters obliquely into another substance, such as water or a stone. The refractive angle is a reliable, useful tool in identifying gemstones.

Another useful tool is the *specific gravity* of a gem, or the expression of the relationship between the weight of a stone and the weight of an equal volume of water. Diamond is 3.5 times heavier than the same volume of water, so its specific gravity is 3.5 The specific gravity of gems varies between 1 and 7. Values under 2 are light (amber is 1.1); those between 2 and 4 are normal (quartz is 2.6); and those above 4 are heavy (galena is 7.4).

Finally, gems are also identified by measuring their *absorption spectrum,* or the bands of color seen through a spectroscope. Each gem has a unique absorption spectrum consisting of broad bands of color interspersed with black vertical lines of differing widths. The absorption spectrum can be used to distinguish between imitation, synthetic, and natural stones. We will discuss this later.

Cutting and Polishing

There are three basic operations in preparing a gemstone from the rough: sawing, grinding, and polishing. The cutting of colored stones is called *lapidary work,* and the cutter is a *lapidary.* A stone is first sawed into shape with a rotating disk of iron or bronze that is impregnated with diamond powder. The coolant is soapy water, oil, or paraffin. The final shape is cut on a vertical, roughly grained carborundum wheel and cooled with water.

In general, there are three different types of cut: the *facet,* the *plain cut,* and the *mixed cut.* The facet cut is applied to transparent stones because the small, even facets give the gem a higher luster and a better play of color. Most facet cuts are built on two basic types. The *brilliant cut,* with 32 or more facets, is used with diamonds and other stones with a high refractive index, to bring out their brilliance. The *emerald,* or *step cut,* features a large central rectangular facet called a *table facet,* which gives a good view of the color of the stone. The faceting of stones is a specialized art first developed around the 15th century, and is enjoyed today by hobbyists as well as professionals.

The *plain cut* is a much simpler process than faceting and is used for agates, opaque stones, and stones with inclusions. The bottom is cut level and the top is either level or, more often, domed. A stone with a domed or rounded top is called a *cabochon* (cab' a shawn). In a *mixed cut* the upper part is level and the lower part is faceted.

Gem Substitutes

These stones are classified as imitations, reconstructed stones, or synthetic stones. *Imitation* stones originated with the Egyptians and are usually made today with glass or plastic. *Reconstructed* stones are made by fusing a piece of natural stone to another piece of artificial material such as glass or foil. For example, fusing two layers of a natural gemstone with colored glue between them like a sandwich, makes a "triplet." An example of a "doublet" would be a colorless beryl crown cemented to a piece of green glass to produce a stone that looks like an emerald. The joint of an assembled or reconstructed stone is often covered by the setting, but will show under magnification. Dyes and plastics are commonly used to impregnate porous gems such as turquoise to make them brighter and more durable.

Synthetic gemstones are identical chemically and structurally to their natural counterparts. They are made by a flame fusion process in which powdered raw material is melted in a furnace at 1,360 degrees Fahrenheit. The molten drops fall onto a cradle, where they crystallize and form a pear-shaped "boule." The gems are then cut from these boules.

The reason gemstones are altered is to make less expensive jewelry. All gems with artificial changes, except for heat-treated stones and dyed agates, must be marked as such when offered for sale. It is wise to check with the dealer to make sure you are getting exactly what you want.

Types of Deposits and Mining

In order to find the natural stones, it helps to know a little about rock formation. There are three major types of rock formations in the Earth: *igneous, sedimentary,* and *metamorphic.* Igneous rocks are the solidification of magma or molten rock over a period of time. Plutonic igneous rocks such as granite and quartz are formed deep below the Earth's surface. Due to their long process of formation, the individual crystals have sufficient time to grow quite large. Volcanic igneous rocks such as obsidian are formed directly from molten rocks that have cooled near the Earth's surface, and are without a visible crystalline structure.

Igneous rocks are generally harder than 5.5, with a crystalline texture of interlocking mineral grains. In general, light-colored igneous rocks are rich in the light-colored minerals: quartz, alkali feldspars, and muscovite mica. Chemically, these rocks have an excess of silica. Dark-colored igneous rocks lack silica, but are rich in iron- and magnesium-bearing minerals, and in the calcium and sodium feldspars. The most common rock-forming minerals are quartz and feldspars.

Many gem minerals are found in *pegmatites,* which are lens-like bodies of more coarsely grained igneous rocks that cut across the finer-grained parent rock. Pegmatites were originally cavities containing gas and residual fluids escaping from the cooling granite magma. These cavities were like wombs in which crystalline structures of various kinds formed over a period of time under high pressure and temperature. Pegmatites, therefore, are excellent sites for mineral and gemstone collecting.

Sedimentary rocks are formed under moderate pressure from layers of accumulated sediment and deposits of organic matter. Sedimentary rocks tend to be layered, and fossils are commonly found in them.

Sandstone and limestone are examples of sedimentary rocks. Sometimes the harder gemstones will be found in the softer sedimentary host rock that has begun to wear away.

Metamorphic rocks are already existing igneous or sedimentary rocks that are subjected to chemical activity, heat, or pressure, which reorganizes their mineral composition. They essentially undergo changes without becoming fluid and are often conspicuously bent or folded. Schist and gneiss are examples of metamorphic rocks. Knowing something about the host rocks can help you know where to look for gemstones.

Mineral Families

A number of gemstones are actually varieties of quartz, feldspar, and other mineral groupings. We will now describe the relevant groupings so that you will understand some similarities in the physical properties of the stones in each grouping.

Quartz, or silicon dioxide, accounts for about 12 percent of the Earth's crust, and can be found in igneous, sedimentary, and metamorphic rocks. The hardness of quartz and its chemical stability under weathering make it the last residue of a great variety of rocks. We can divide the quartz family into several groupings:

1. *Macrocrystalline quartz* grows in veins or cavities that are partially filled with silica. Under favorable conditions in pegmatite, crystals of clear, smoky, or amethyst quartz can grow to several hundred pounds. This group of quartz, with the exception of rose quartz, is commonly found in the familiar form of six sides and a termination point. These quartzes are named according to their color:

   ◆ Amethyst: pale violet to deep purple.

   ◆ Clear quartz: sometimes called rock crystal, clear.

   ◆ Citrine: clear yellow, golden yellow.

   ◆ Smoky quartz: smoky or grayish brown to black.

   ◆ Rose quartz: pink.

   ◆ Black tourmalinated quartz: clear quartz with inclusions of black tourmaline.

   ◆ Rutilated quartz: clear or smoky quartz with needle-like inclusions of rutile.

2. In the chalcedony or *microcrystalline* quartz group, the silica forms compact masses of tiny crystals, which are dull, rather than glassy, in appearance. Generally, microcrystalline quartz is formed near the surface of the Earth, where temperatures and pressures are relatively lower. Here are the microcrystalline quartzes that are included in this book:

    ◆   Aventurine: quartz colored with iridescent green mica.

    ◆   Chalcedony: white, blue, or gray. (We describe the white chalcedony in this book.)

    ◆   Chrysoprase: opaque apple green.

    ◆   Bloodstone: opaque dark green with spots of red jasper (also called heliotrope).

    ◆   Carnelian: translucent red, orange, or yellow.

    ◆   Moss agate: translucent milky white with moss-like green incusions of hornblende.

    ◆   Tiger's Eye: gold-yellow to gold-brown layers.

3. The *agates* are quartzes of the microcrystalline type that have a concentric banded structure. Agates are usually found in volcanic rocks. Sometimes they are stained chemically to make their colors brighter:

    ◆   Blue lace agate: light blue and white layers.

    ◆   Fire agate: various shades of brown layers.

4. The *feldspar* make up the largest group of minerals and are found in all volcanic rocks. The colors in granite come from its feldspar content. Feldspars are slightly softer than quartz, registering about 6 on the Mohs' scale. There are sub-groupings of feldspars, based on cleavage and chemical composition, depending on whether they are potassium aluminum silicates or sodium calcium silicates. This book includes:

    ◆   Amazonite: opaque blue-green, light turquoise (sometimes called amazon stone).

    ◆   Moonstone: colorless or milky to faintly yellow, will show a silvery blue sheen in reflected light.

    ◆   Labradorite: gray with brilliant iridescent colors at certain angles in reflected light.

    ◆   Orange sunstone: red-orange or red-brown with metallic glitter (sometimes called aventurine feldspar).

- Yellow orthoclase feldspar: translucent yellow (sometimes called yellow sunstone).

5. *Corundum* is normally found in a type of marble formed from limestone, which has been subjected to metamorphic action. Corundum has a Mohs' standard of 9 and is prized for its hard durability and brilliant colors when faceted. We include:

   - Ruby: red.
   - Sapphire: colors other than red, such as blue and clear.

6. The *beryl* gemstones, with a hardness of 7 1/2-8, are among the most widely known and differ in color only, due to the presence of trace elements. We include:

   - Emerald: rich green.
   - Aquamarine: light blue, light blue-green.

Chapter 2

SPIRITUAL ASPECTS
OF GEMSTONES

I f you are reading this book you may already have been to your local rock shop and stood in awe of the beautiful colors and patterns in the stones. It is possible you enjoy the smooth solidity of a beach pebble and the way it connects you with the earth. Whatever path you are traveling, you may have decided that it is now time to reconnect with the Earth and to experience its wisdom at deeper levels.

In order to understand the wisdom of stones, you need to begin to perceive all life as different frequencies and forms of *energy*. This energy can be experienced at the physical, emotional, mental, and spiritual levels. In this chapter we will review the concept of life-force energy and the human energy system. We will then become more attuned to the spiritual levels of reality, where life-force energy creates and balances our natural physical world. We will talk about how our individual journeys to discover the meaning of life influence our perceptions of the life-force energies in gemstones. Finally, we will describe how you can choose and care for your gemstones.

Reviewing Life-force Energy and the Human Energy System

Everything in Nature consists of life-force energy vibrating at different levels. On the physical level, life-force energy ultimately becomes matter. On the spiritual level, life-force energy is Consciousness expressed as qualities such as courage, joy, and compassion. Life-force energy is known to have healing qualities, and it is these spiritual healing qualities that we seek in the stones. Your thoughts also have varying amounts of life-force energy, depending on how positive they are. When you combine the life-force energy in conscious positive thoughts or affirmations with the life-force energy of the stones, the healing potential is greater than the energy of either the thoughts or stones separately.

Your body is a complex energy system. The *aura,* or energy field, surrounding your body is composed of several layers or *subtle bodies.* Our working system roughly defines three layers, which correspond to the physical, emotional-mental, and spiritual levels of development. We combine the emotional and mental levels together, as they both influence the creation of conscious beliefs.

The physical layer is usually called the *etheric body* and extends out about one-quarter inch to two or three inches from the physical body. Being the densest layer, it is the easiest to perceive and is sometimes seen as a thin band of white or grayish light. When you wear or place stones on your body you are directly affecting the etheric body, which serves as a blue-print for the physical body.

Surrounding the etheric body are the *emotional and mental* subtle bodies. We sense these layers from three or four inches to about 12 inches above the body. These fields are often seen clairvoyantly as shimmering, changing colors that indicate the emotional and mental state of a person's thoughts.

The *spiritual subtle body* extends from about 12 inches to two or three feet from the physical body. This is the level where you merge with your Higher Self and are connected with the reality beyond your conscious awareness.

Your subtle bodies are highly sensitive to thought forms. When a thought form enters one of your subtle bodies, the structure of that body changes to resonate with the thought. Depending on the nature of the thought, the subtle body either becomes more stable, structured, and filled with life-force energy, or more disorganized. This process happens quickly and spontaneously with your passing thoughts. That is why clairvoyants often see many colors, including predominant overtones, as well as various changing colors. Your very being is structured by thoughts. Therefore, you can use positive thoughts to affect your sensitive energy fields to bring about balance.

In addition to serving as both a blueprint for the body and a record of your experiences, the subtle bodies also serve as transducers of life-force energy. As you receive life-force energy from a variety of sources, including thought, it is stepped down at each level and made into a grosser, or denser, form that your body can use.

The *chakras* form another component of your energy system. The chakras are energy vortexes, or "wheels of light," which both connect the subtle bodies and act as transducers for life-force energy. There are seven major chakras, associated with the major endocrine glands. The chakras represent physical, emotional, mental, and spiritual levels of development. As you evolve in understanding both your interdependence with others as well as the Oneness of All Life, your chakras receive more life-force energies at increasingly finer frequencies. The levels of development represented by each chakra, and their locations on the human body, are summarized in Figures 3-1 and 3-2 at the end of Chapter 3.

The thymus gland, a less understood component of the human energy system, receives and directs life-force energies. It is located in the middle of the chest between the breasts and the hollow of the throat (See Figure 3-1). The thymus gland was originally thought to have no function at all because it seems to atrophy in many people after the age of 13. It is now generally known that the thymus gland shrinks during serious illness and severe physical stress.

The thymus gland is more clearly understood in terms of its spiritual function. It is a very sensitive gland and is activated by *positive mental attitudes*. Apparently, it remains largely dormant unless you consciously practice giving and receiving Unconditional Love, with the realization that your thoughts affect your body. However, once you welcome Unconditional Love in the form of positive thoughts and spiritual understanding into your life, the thymus gland is activated to do two things. First, it acts as a sensor that detects where an imbalance of life-force energy is occurring in the body. Second, apparently it can transduce the life-force energy of thought and direct it for rebalancing the physical body. Thus, it monitors and regulates the body's immune system when the mind-body connection is understood. The thymus gland is discussed again in Chapter 7.

The energy system of the body reflects the electromagnetic properties of life-force energy. One side of the body and one hand carry a negative electrical charge and a north pole magnetic charge. In this book, we call the negative hand the *receiving hand.* The other side of the body and the opposite hand carry a positive charge and a south pole magnetic charge. We call the positive hand the *sending hand.* To determine your sending and receiving hands, you will need two single-pointed clear quartz crystals:

1. Place one crystal in your hand, with the point facing toward your body, and the other in your opposite hand, with the point toward your fingertips. Be aware of how your energy is moving in your body. Is there a flow?

2. Now point each crystal in the opposite direction, reversing the circuit. Check your energy again. Is there a flow now?

One circuit will often feel more open than the other will. The hand in which the crystal points toward the body becomes your *receiving hand* and the hand in which the crystal points away from your body becomes your *sending hand.* When you wish to receive energy from a stone or meditate with it, hold it in your receiving hand. If you want to work with others, hold the stone in your sending hand.

Either your receiving hand or your sending hand can be your *sensing hand.* To determine your sensing hand you will need a single crystal:

1. Hold your hands about four inches apart, as if you were holding an imaginary ball, with the crystal in your right hand. The point is facing the left palm.

2. Draw circles in the field in front of the left palm.

3. Repeat with the crystal in the left hand pointing toward the right palm.

The sensations will be stronger and more pronounced in your *sensing* hand. Hold a stone in your sensing hand when you want to understand its energy or to check if it needs cleaning or charging. You also work with your sensing hand to check the energy field surrounding the body of someone you are working on.

The Spiritual Reality of the Devic Kingdoms of Nature

Just as you learn to perceive life-force energy in your own system, you can learn to perceive life-force energy in the Kingdoms of Nature. All of Nature exists in physical forms that you experience with your five senses, as well as in spiritual forms, which are part of the larger reality. The Kingdoms of Nature can teach you about the spiritual dimensions of physical reality and the Divine Source that is present in all life.

Just as you have a Higher Self that is able to share universal wisdom and guide you in ways that you can understand, each mineral also has a "Higher Self" called a *Deva*. The information that follows is channeled from a Clear Quartz Crystal Deva, which is one level of Deva that works with a particular species or form:

> *Let me tell you some things about myself and the Devic Kingdom. My Kingdom is based in the world of Spirit. We are Light Beings with light bodies that are essentially formless, although we are capable of taking on form. Our Will is the Will of the Divine and we communicate directly with the Divine Source. That is the same as your being with your Higher Self.*

> *Everything consists of life-force energy. As a Crystal Deva one of my purposes is to create a blueprint for the physical crystal form from life-force energy. I am like an architect, working with the material of life-force energy to create a unique form. I am also like a manager in that I work with the life-force energies to maintain an ongoing, optimal balance in the crystals I work with. This balance is always changing, as the crystals give and receive according to their own needs, and I keep the life-force energies flowing in a stabilized manner.*

Another level of Devas we call Overlighting Devas. Their purpose is to maintain a stable flow and balance of life-force energies in a geographical area or among groups of forms. The Overlighting Deva of the Mineral Kingdom talks with us about what we can learn from the Kingdom of Nature:

> First of all, you need to work co-creatively with Nature in order to survive. We do not see the Kingdoms of Nature as separate from the Human Kingdom as you do. We see the connection and interdependence of all life and we wish to share this message with you in as many ways as we can. The process of maintaining balance for planet Earth emphasizes interdependence. You cannot live without the energy received from the sun, which the Plant Kingdom gives to you in a usable form. The life that a life form releases as a gift of service is a growth enhancer for another Kingdom. You can learn about any Kingdom of Nature by linking your being with it.

> It is important for you to see yourselves as a positive part of the balancing process of the planet. Plants, animals, and minerals willingly give their life-force energies for your rebalancing. Whenever you are "drawn" to a certain stone, your Higher Self is telling you that you can benefit from the qualities of that stone. You need only listen to your intuitive guidance. As you better understand how to heal your sickness with your thoughts and the healing energies of Nature, you will strengthen the vitality of the entire planet.

> All of life operates first at a very dense level of matter and at very specific frequencies, and continues to evolve until it reaches the stage where it can work creatively with broad frequencies of formless energy. In this evolutionary cycle, the Human Kingdom is not the highest form of life. You are learning to bring your own will into union with the Divine Will. You are learning to focus both your emotional being and your thoughts in order to bring about what you are seeking. When your will is in harmony with Divine Will you can move into the spiritual realm, where you work with your creative capacities in Oneness with the Universal.

We Devas can share with you from our perspective of the Universal Oneness. Whenever you seek to learn from any member of the Mineral Kingdom, you need to release all sense of judgment as it relates to us or to the wisdom that we share. Communication becomes difficult when you approach us with the sense that you are truly the all-knowing ones. You ask why we wait for the Human Kingdom to initiate contact with us. The answer is that for us to contact you requires an expenditure of life-force energies that we prefer to direct in balancing and harmonizing the planet's life-force energies. You must use your will to seek contact with us.

You must also learn to release self-judgment and exercise the qualities of acceptance and patience as they relate to the communication that you receive from us. Each time that you seek to enter our dimensionless space and are harboring judgment about your ability to receive, at the moment in time you have blocked the path for communication to take place. We are aware of when you are in the space of internal struggle and doubt, whether it relates to us or the material that is being shared. I say, trust that the process of learning is evolving and becoming more pure. Each time we come together, we harmonize the energies between your Kingdom and mine.

One of our functions is to step down life-force energies from the Masters and from other levels of reality into forms that you humans can understand and work with in your thoughts and in your physical bodies. Your physical world serves as an embodiment of spiritual truths that you perceive with your five senses and your human form. The Kingdoms of Nature teach you not only to see with physical eyes, but to expand in your awareness beyond the limitations of physical form. We Devas are therefore a "Light Bridge" for you to understand your Oneness. Be open to the Light that the Kingdoms of Nature have to share with you. We of the Devic Kingdom give our service to you joyfully. Feel the peace of our presence.

Here are some ways you can begin to attune to the Devic Kingdom through your gemstones:

1. Holding your gemstones, breathe deeply, relax your body, and mentally go to a natural place where you feel safe and totally at peace. Affirm that your Higher Self is with you and remain receptive for a few minutes.

2. Now focus your awareness on the gemstone in your hand. Thank the God/Goddess/All That Is for the gemstone's being and express your gratitude for the gifts of the Earth.

3. Look upon your stone with humility and respect, as a friend who can teach you and help you. Affirm that the Deva of your stone is now with you and wait receptively. See if you can notice the energy shift from your Higher Self to the Deva. You may feel a sense of calm joy, or perhaps another energy sensation, such as a specific visual pattern of colors.

 In your mind you can repeat the process by first calling your Higher Self and then the Deva, so that you can clarify the energy differences in your being.

4. Ask the Deva to share the guidance you need from the stone and allow yourself to receive it. If you would like to clarify what you receive, you can ask yes/no questions using the pendulum. You might ask, "Are you helping to restore physical vitality to my body?" or "Am I to carry you with me?"

5. Thank the Deva and the stone for their help and love. Every stone has a gift to offer the Human Kingdom. You merely need to be patient and persistent in learning to adjust our spiritual energy to that of the stone. The Devas very much wish to work with us; it is primarily a matter of establishing an "open line" and an intuitive language. Once you have linked with the stone on a spiritual level, you do not always need to be in an altered state of consciousness to consciously receive from the stone. As you deepen your spiritual awareness, you will find that you receive from the stone in your own unique ways.

The Influence of Beliefs upon Our Perceptions of Gemstone Qualities

When you sense the non-physical properties of a stone, your conscious beliefs have a direct impact on what you perceive. As humans we have a range of skills and abilities related to our purpose in life. Each of us in our unique way has the opportunity to serve in the overall balance. Stones also have a range of qualities or attributes related to their purpose in being and the service that they give. They have both a physical and a spiritual purpose. Physically, they are a foundation for all of life. Spiritually, each stone is an expression of Consciousness or Love, and exists in complete Oneness with All That Is. However, the manner in which we humans experience this Oneness differs according to our individual religious and cultural training. *When you work with stones, you interpret their Consciousness according to* your *own spiritual understanding.* You tend toward consistency in your belief systems and consequently, you do one of two things: either you interpret your perceptions in a manner consistent with other things that you know and understand, or you dismiss the perception from your conscious mind. In the past the spiritual qualities of stones were not understood and were dismissed as "magic."

Your beliefs affect your perception of events. For example, many of you who never noticed "coincidences" before may later come to realize that they are guidance from your intuition. Then you begin to notice many coincidences that were actually happening all along, without your awareness. In this way you become aware of how your beliefs create your reality.

Your relationships with stones and all the Kingdoms of Nature are interdependent ones. You relate to the stones according to your purpose in being. Those of you who are involved in helping others heal their physical bodies may relate to stones according to their physical healing properties. Those who work with emotional and spiritual healing may relate to the spiritual healing aspects of the stones. You understand the stones according to how you perceive them as helping you fulfill your purpose.

Your physical and emotional well-being affects your sensitivity to the stones. If your body is out of balance from drugs, alcohol, or stimulants, or your emotions are in a state of imbalance, you will be less sensitive to the energies of the stones. Once you undertake a program of physical well-being, not only is it easier for you to sense the qualities of gemstones, but you can allow them to work to their maximum energy potential. Physical well-being includes a healthy diet, exercise, the cleansing of toxins, and an emotionally nurturing environment.

Your "body constitution" also influences how you perceive gemstone energy. Someone who is very physically active, with an outgoing, expressive nature, may find an active, energetic stone such as ruby to be balancing and maybe even soothing. Someone else, with a quieter, gentler, less active constitution, might find ruby highly stimulating and may find that rose quartz feels more balancing.

When you look at a stone, your first perceptions may be related to its color. Therefore, you interpret its energy according to your experiences with color. For example, I relate to orange as a stimulating color and tend to experience orange carnelian as a dynamic stone. Jonathan relates to orange in terms of warmth and often experiences orange carnelian as a warm, gently expanding stone.

The way in which you move through the lessons of your life affects your perceptions. Once, in a workshop, we had two people describe their experiences with malachite. One person was not happy with it at all and could not wait to put it down. A second woman was quite comfortable with malachite and had a sense that she needed to hold onto it. Our experience with malachite is that it has an intense quality, which can rapidly focus your awareness on fear that you need to release. The first person was not in a place to look at emotional change at that time. She enjoyed and needed the stones at the workshop that felt gentle and grounding to her. The second woman was very comfortable with the intensity of malachite and was in the middle of an emotional transition. You are drawn to the stones that are best for you at any given time.

Gemstone Correlations: Astrology and Other Metaphysical Belief Systems

There are many different associations that people have made between gemstones, the planets, and the signs of the Zodiac. The planets and stars, like everything else in Nature, have spiritual qualities to which you are particularly receptive at the time of your birth. Your astrological natal chart is a description of how the qualities of the planets and signs of the Zodiac are interwoven to help shape both your outer and inner natures. The spiritual qualities of the planets and signs are perceived intuitively, and therefore, are related to the beliefs and experiences of the person describing them. Thus the associations of gemstones with signs and planets are subjective, individual, and based on linking similar qualities according to a certain perceptual framework.

If you are already attuned to the system of astrology, or for that matter, numerology, tarot, or the Kabbalah, you can use the elements of your system to understand the healing qualities of the stones. As you merge your system with the use of stones, you will attain a broader knowledge of the stones and find new ways to work them into your system.

It is important to remember that there are many reasons why descriptions of gemstone qualities are so different. You should honor the varying experiences you share with each other. It is best to form your own relationships with the stones and trust your perceptions and beliefs. *Understand that what* you *read is truth for the person or persons who wrote it and that* you *are in the process of expanding your own truth. At all times honor and learn from your own perceptions.*

Choosing Gemstones

When you go to purchase gemstones you will find them offered in three major forms: *rough, polished* or *tumbled,* and *faceted.* Each form has its advantages and disadvantages and it is entirely a matter of personal preference which form you choose. Rough stones found at gem shows and lapidary shops are large in size, unshaped by humans, and quite inexpensive. Polished stones, also found at gem shows and rock shops, come in two shapes. The cabochons are often oval, flat on the bottom, and domed on top. Polished or tumbled stones, which are more rounded, have been shaped in machines called tumblers. The stone is placed in water in the tumbler along with finer and finer grades of grit, while the tumbler motor agitates the stone. Polished stones show the intricate nuances of the colors within them better than rough stones and are also inexpensive. Faceted stones, found at gem shows and jewelry stores, are cut to reflect light and their colors are usually brilliant and clear. They are much more expensive than either rough or polished stones.

You have to decide how you personally feel about stones that have been shaped by humans. Lapidaries who work with an eye only on profit will add a different energy to the stone than those who work with an attitude of honor and love. A great deal of stone is "wasted" in the cutting process and discarded. On the other hand, a skilled artist with love and knowledge of the stone can create a true gift of beauty and service. Ultimately, the energy of a gemstone is a blend of your beliefs, your love for the stone, and the energy of the stone itself, as well as the energy of those who have been significantly involved with it.

When choosing gemstones, try to be guided by your intuition as much as possible. If you ask for the appropriate guidance, Nature will always guide you to what you need. When you are attracted to the color of a particular stone, or you keep thinking about it after seeing it, your intuition is probably telling you that you can benefit from the qualities of that stone. When you are choosing a stone, relax, breathe deeply, and put yourself in touch with a sense of reverence and gratitude. In this way you will be open and receptive for guidance to come to you.

Caring for Gemstones

Gemstones, like clear quartz crystals, need to be cleared and charged. Over a period of time, gemstones can collect various forms of negative or static energies such as negative thought forms and emotions, electronic pollution, and other imbalanced electromagnetic energies. These energies can affect the emanation of positive vibratory energy. It is important to clean and charge a gemstone when you first obtain it, and frequently thereafter, to keep it at its highest level of functioning. As you charge the stones they begin to attune to your energies because you are involved in the process.

Some signs that a gemstone needs to be cleaned are a sense of decreased energy coming from it, an increased cloudiness within it, or a stickiness to the touch. There are many ways to clean a gemstone, so choose the method that seems right for you.

For *quick cleaning* after healing work or at the end of the day, hold the gemstone under cold running water, for half a minute or more. Visualize White Light clearing and illuminating the gemstone.

Burn dried sage leaves in a piece of pottery or abalone shell. You can buy sage leaves at an herb or health food store. Pass the gemstone through the fragrant smoke, affirming that the gemstone is being purified. You can also soak gemstones in sage tea. Sage has the ability to both clear and uplift the emotional, mental, and spiritual states, which is one reason it was used by Native Americans as a purifier at the beginning of spiritual ceremonies.

Use your breath to clear the gemstone. When you breathe, you inhale and exhale life-force energy. For this reason, the breath is a powerful tool for healing:

> Hold your gemstone and inhale the vitality of pure Light.
>
> Hold your breath while you affirm that this Light is clearing and charging your gemstone.
>
> Continue this thought focus while you exhale slowly through your nostrils onto the crystal.
>
> You will need to do this several times until the gemstone feels like it has been cleared.

Soak your gemstones in a salt-water solution for overnight or longer. We have used anywhere from half a teaspoon, to one-quarter cup sea salt, to two cups of spring water. It is safer not to use this method with malachite, azurite, and other minerals containing copper, because they can lose their polished sheen.

Bury your gemstones in sea salt for one to seven days. Sea salt attracts imbalanced energies like a magnet. Throw the salt away after you have cleaned your gemstones. This method is okay to use with malachite and azurite.

Bury your gemstone in the Earth for several days. Ask the Devas of the gemstone and the Earth to help you transform the imbalanced energy.

Place your stones outside during rain, snow, or thunderstorms. These weather conditions help rebalance the energy of the stones.

Ask the Devas to assist in clearing and charging your stones. As we have learned how to work with the Devas, we have come to better understand how much they can help us in healing co-creatively. Currently we clear and charge our gemstones in the following manner:

1. Place the stone or stones in a bowl of water.

2. Become still within and merge with the healing energy of the Earth itself.

3. Ask the Devas of the Mineral Kingdom to help in clearing and charging the stones. You can visualize them being transformed in the vitality of Earth's core.

4. After a couple of minutes, or when you sense that the process has ended, thank the Devas for their help and, if possible, leave the bowl outside for several hours or more.

After clearing your gemstones, you can further *charge their energies by leaving them outside in the sun or in the full moon.* You can also place your stones under a pyramid, if you have one. A charged stone gives off a dynamic "electric" quality that you can usually discern in various parts of your body. The more a stone loses its charge, the less you will feel its energy in your body. We like to have more than one piece of particular gemstone, so that we have one to work with while the others are clearing and charging. When you have finished a clearing and charging process, remember to thank the stone for its service to you.

There is no single "correct" way to clear and charge your gemstones. The methods you choose are based on your beliefs and your perceptions of energy. You must decide intuitively which method to use, how long to leave them, and when they are again rebalanced.

Asking for Intuitive Guidance

Here is a way to use your breath and the gemstone in order to receive intuitive impressions.

1. Sit and hold the gemstone on your Third Eye.

2. Take deep, diaphragmatic breaths to balance and center yourself.

3. Inhale deeply and ask your question. For example, "What is the best way to clean this gemstone?"

4. Pause and hold your breath, keeping your focus on your intent, or a mental picture of your intent. Holding your breath helps to build the power of the life-force energy.

5. Exhale, relax, and let the thought go. You may think that it is necessary to keep directing your will in order to manifest intent. A crucial step in working with Spirit is to *listen*, which is the point of relaxing deeply.

6. Pause, and allow information about your question to come to you. If you do not receive the information you asked for the first time, try to release any preconceived ideas about the answer, or about the form the answer might take. Then try again and create a rhythm of focusing and letting go.

How to Use the Crystal Pendulum

Another way to learn how to dialogue with your Higher Guidance is through a pendulum, which serves as a type of biofeedback device. By listening to your Higher Self as you go about your daily life, you can learn to fine-tune your discrimination in energy sensing. You can dialogue with a pendulum made with any material. In this instance, we have chosen to use a crystal pendulum because clear quartz crystal can amplify the energy of your intent.

Before using a pendulum, it helps to carry the crystal with you for a few days to attune it to your energy. When you are ready to begin, you can sit down at a table and hold the chain or cord of the pendulum with your thumb, index, and middle fingers. Your elbow should be resting comfortably on the table and your wrist straight. Experiment with the length of the chain or cord. A comfortable length will be between three and 12 inches. In our experience, the material of the chain or cord doesn't really matter.

It is very important to be relaxed and centered when using the pendulum. Take a few deep breaths and visualize a place where you feel totally at peace. Affirm that your Higher Self is with you. Don't rush this relaxation. If you are not relaxed you will not get clear answers. In the beginning it is easy to become so worried about whether or not the pendulum will work that you can block the movement of the pendulum with your tension.

When you are ready, ask the pendulum to show you the movement for "yes" and the movement for "no." If you get no response, try holding the pendulum over the positive and then negative ends of a battery (not a dead one). You can use the movement over the positive end for "yes" and the movement over the negative end for "no." If this method does not work for you, don't despair. You can decide on a system such as clockwise (yes) and counterclockwise (no), or vertical (yes) and horizontal (no), or a combination of these positions.

Move the pendulum in your "yes" direction, visualizing "yes" in bold letters in your mind, and connecting to the sensation of the "yes" motion. Affirm that this is a "yes." Repeat with the "no" motion. Then ask your pendulum to show you a "yes" or a "no." This may take some practice over a period of time. It took me about two weeks to become comfortable with using the pendulum. Trust that you are learning, and persevere until you get a response.

Now you are ready to begin asking questions that can be answered with a "yes" or a "no." When you are working with a pendulum, do not have your arms or legs crossed or touching each other. It is also good to wash your hands before starting. Work on an uncluttered surface, away from electrical equipment and magnets.

Ask your pendulum, "Are we in harmony?" or "Am I in tune with my pendulum?" Readings are easily influenced by fatigue, illness, an emotional state of mind, beliefs regarding the question, and any inharmonious energies that may be present. Learning to stay in harmony with your pendulum is one of the most challenging lessons in working with it.

As you receive answers, listen to your inner voice. Watch for bodily sensations and inner perceptual sensations. We both get an uncomfortable pressure in our hands or an inner sensation of blocked energy when the answer is "no."

You are able to gain additional information by noting the strength of the pendulum's responses, particularly in healing work. In addition, you may be able to receive responses from the pendulum different from your standard yes/no movement. At this time it would be a good idea to ask your pendulum to indicate how it would move to communicate each of the following statements:

1. Now is not the appropriate time to ask that question.

2. I am not in tune with the pendulum.

3. I need to clarify my question and ask it in a different way.

Questions to Ask Your Crystal Pendulum

Now you are ready to use your pendulum in gemstone work. Here are questions that can be answered with the pendulum. Ask them in a yes/no format. Some of these questions refer to ways of working with a gemstone that will be discussed in later chapters.

Choosing Your Gemstone

1. "Am I to work with you?" ("You" refers to a gemstone.)
2. "Are you to be used in meditation/healing?"

Care of Your Gemstone

1. There are two ways you can find out whether a gemstone needs to be cleaned. One is to hold the pendulum over the gemstone and ask the pendulum to show you its relative strength. If you get a no response, the crystal needs to be cleaned. Another way is to ask the crystal "Do you need to be cleaned?"

2. Get a yes/no response for each of the following methods of cleaning crystals to find out how your gemstone needs to be cleaned:
   - Burying in sea salt.
   - Soaking in sea salt water.
   - Holding in sage smoke.
   - Breathing on it.
   - Putting gemstone out in the rain.
   - Holding gemstone under running water.
   - Burying gemstone underground.

3. When you have had some practice with the pendulum, you can make an arc, and ask the pendulum to point to the optimal way to clean the particular gemstone in the shortest period of time. Using an arc will save you time, as well.

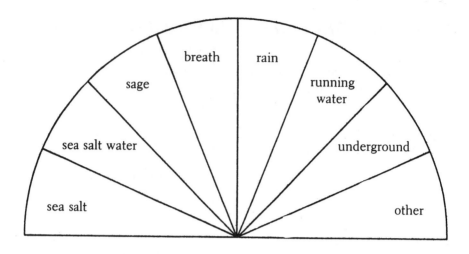

Figure 2-1. Pendulum arc for specific qualities.

4. Ask whether the gemstone should be cleaned for four hours, six hours, eight hours, overnight, 24 hours"

5. Recheck the gemstone and ask, "Have you been adequately cleaned?" Sense the gemstone with your hand. You can eventually learn by touch when the crystal is clean.

6. Ask: "How is the gemstone to be charged?"

    By using:
    - Affirmations?
    - Breath?
    - Sunlight?
    - On a cluster?
    - Under a pyramid?
    - In a thunderstorm?
    - For how long?

There are many ways that you can expand your work with the pendulum, and we hope that we have stimulated your exploration in this area. The most important thing to remember is to remain centered and relaxed. By learning to sense when you may be influencing the results, you will become more in harmony with your Higher Will.

Saturation

Our experience has been that over a period of time a gemstone will absorb imbalanced energy, which diminishes its capacity to generate balanced life-force energy. This seems to be particularly true of gemstones that are used for healing purposes. One sign to look for is that the gemstone will feel like it needs to be cleaned, except that cleaning it does not seem to clear and regenerate the energy. Another sign is when a gemstone that first felt uplifting or comfortable begins to feel uncomfortable. When this happens, the stone has done all it can, and it is time to return it to the earth (or the water).

1. Ask the Spiritual Consciousness of the gemstone whether its work with you has been completed, or whether it has a further purpose in your life.

2. Ask it what Element (Earth or Water primarily) will be most beneficial for its internal balance, and take the gemstone where it needs to go. Most likely it will be a natural place.

3. When you release the gemstone, take a few minutes in meditation to thank it for the service it has given you, and honor your interdependence with the Earth.

Gemstones appreciate being treated with care and love. As you work with them, you will become more sensitive to their needs, and they will reward you with expanding awareness.

Chapter 3

LEARNING ABOUT GEM ENERGY: COLOR, SOUND, AND CHAKRA AFFINITIES

I n this chapter we will begin the process of experiencing the spiritual qualities of gemstones by observing them from several perspectives: color and sound, as well as chakra and subtle body affinities. By perceiving gemstone qualities through different perceptual frameworks, you can increase your understanding of their versatility. You also sharpen your own intuitive skills and find which perspectives are most natural to you.

Life-force energies can be perceived through the mediums of color and sound. We will first discuss correspondences of gemstone energy and the spiritual qualities of colors. Our second perspective in learning about gem energy is sound. By sensitizing yourself to sound, you can learn to find a stone's dominant frequency, or *soul tone*. The soul tone, similar to a stone's color, is a key to understanding its spiritual qualities and the particular gifts it has to offer.

Our third perspective in learning about gem energy involves learning to sense a stone's affinities for various chakras and subtle bodies. Each stone has an individual purpose or gift to give, just as each of us has a particular purpose in being. For this reason each stone will show an affinity for particular chakras and subtle bodies in your energy field.

Perspective 1: Color

We have previously stated that life-force energy has physical, emotional, mental, and spiritual qualities that are expressed by all living things, including gemstones. We can further state that color and sound are defined in physical terms as different expressions of the same healing life-force energy. On the spiritual level, it is possible to sense color as sound and sound as color. Let us now look at color as a way of understanding the qualities of gemstones.

All light is visible radiant energy that travels through space in the form of waves. It travels 186,000 miles per second in varying wavelengths. At the cosmic end of the scale, wavelengths are so short that millions of waves placed end to end will fit within an area the size of a postage stamp. At the opposite end of the spectrum the largest waves may exceed 100,000 miles in length. Located near the middle of the spectrum is the tiny band of radiant energy that is visible to the human eye—the color spectrum.

In Indian philosophy the spiritual qualities of color are closely linked to the seven major chakras; this is the system we work with.

Red

Red, associated with the root chakra, is an intense, focused vibration that builds vitality on the physical level. On the emotional and mental levels, red gives courage and perseverance. On the spiritual level, red strengthens the will and helps you affirm your basic existence as a unique individual.

AFFIRMATION: "WITH RED, I MOVE FORWARD IN LIFE WITH COURAGE AND CONFIDENCE."

Orange

Orange, associated with the lower abdomen chakra, is a warm, expansive vibration that energizes on the physical level.

On the emotional and mental levels, orange stimulates optimism and hope, which makes it a good antidote for fear and depression. On the spiritual level, its expansive quality encourages you to broaden your experience in order to expand who you are.

AFFIRMATION: "WITH ORANGE, I EXPAND MY OPTIMISM AND FAITH."

Yellow

Yellow, associated with the solar plexus chakra, is a light that stimulates vibration on the physical level. On the emotional and mental levels, its sunny qualities include joy, optimism, and confidence. Yellow expands your understanding by fine-tuning your decision-making mind and uplifting you to broader perspectives. It is associated with problem-solving, inventiveness, and, on the spiritual level, joy in being alive.

AFFIRMATION: "WITH YELLOW, I BRING JOY, MENTAL CLARITY, AND CONFIDENCE TO ALL THAT I DO."

Green

Green is associated with the heart chakra and has an affinity with the physical body and the Earth. Physically, it is soothing and balancing. On the emotional and mental levels, green encourages the resolution of conflict through compassion and self-acceptance. Green is also associated with gratitude and material expansion; perhaps because green is the predominant color of the abundance of Nature. Spiritually, green encourages you to trust in the process of growth.

AFFIRMATION: "WITH GREEN, I FLOW WITH EMOTIONAL BALANCE AND HARMONY."

Blue

Blue is associated with the throat chakra and, similar to green, is physically calming and relaxing. On the emotional and mental levels, blue gives qualities of idealism, devotion, and understanding as you begin to express your purpose and aspirations in life.

On the spiritual level, blue can add perspective to your experience through its elevating and peaceful qualities.

AFFIRMATION: "WITH BLUE, I AM STEADY, CALM, AND AT PEACE."

Indigo

Indigo, associated with the third eye chakra, is a deep blue tinged with violet, like the color of the twilight sky. Indigo is a very light, cooling vibration attuned to the spiritual subtle body. Indigo gives an expanded understanding of your everyday world by lifting you into the world of Spirit.

AFFIRMATION: "WITH INDIGO, MY INNER SENSITIVITY TO ALL LIFE EXPANDS AND BECOMES CLEARER."

Violet

Violet, associated with the crown chakra, is even lighter, cooler, and more subtle. Spiritually, it helps you transcend and transform your experience so that you feel a sense of Unity with All. It stimulates qualities of truth, devotion, and responsibility. Violet also helps you let go of beliefs that keep you feeling separated from others.

AFFIRMATION: "WITH VIOLET, I GO BEYOND MY PERSONAL EXISTENCE TO BECOME A PART OF ALL THAT IS."

Pink

Pink works particularly well with the emotional and spiritual subtle bodies and is often associated with the heart chakra. It has a lighter vibration than green and gives qualities of delight, compassion, playfulness, and self-acceptance.

AFFIRMATION: "WITH PINK, I ENJOY BEING WHO I AM."

It is important to develop your own intuitive sense of the colors and their qualities. Here are several ways that you can do this:

1. Focus your awareness on the colors in your daily life. The colors of your clothing can have a healing effect if you take time to merge with them and affirm their qualities. You can choose clothing intuitively on the basis of what you need.

2. When you want to understand how you really feel about something, use oil pastels, watercolors, or Magic Markers, etc., and draw in color. Let yourself express freely on paper, and then go back and notice what colors you used. You will learn a lot about how you relate personally to colors.

3. Work with visualizations in color. When you wish to relax, visualize the woods or the meadow in as much color detail as you can. Visualize sunsets and sunrises, or make up your fantasies in Technicolor. Visualizing colors in your mind helps strengthen your subconscious attunement to color.

4. Work with color meditations.

   a. Inhale while visualizing red expanding from your diaphragm. Hold your breath briefly and focus on red, then slowly exhale red throughout your body. Continue through the rest of the spectrum, breathing three or more times for each color. You can pause after each color and be aware of how each color affects you.

   b. Do a chakra color meditation, breathing red into your root chakra, orange into your lower abdomen, and so on through the color spectrum.

   c. An interesting variation is to choose one chakra, particularly a chakra in which you tend to block energy, and breathe each color into that chakra. Observe which colors seem to affect this chakra.

   d. Another system you might use in breathing color into the chakras comes from Bernard Gunther's *Energy Ecstasy*.[1] This system gives some other interesting insights into the relationship of color and the chakras, which we found useful in understanding chakra placements for gemstones:

root chakra	red-orange
lower abdomen chakra	pink
solar plexus chakra	kelly green
heart chakra	yellow-gold
throat chakra	sky blue
third eye chakra	indigo
crown chakra	purple

It is important to note here that at times each chakra will benefit from a variety of colors. The color associated with a chakra has certain qualities that are relevant to the developmental issues of that chakra. When working intuitively with color, be open to giving any area of your body whatever color it needs. You will broaden your understanding of color and gemstones as well.

Now you are ready to work with the gemstones:

1. If possible, have a friend place a gemstone in your hand without your looking at it.

2. Try to sense what you are experiencing on all levels. Observe your perceptions.

Then look at the stone, sense it again, and be aware of any added perceptions that you receive from the color. How did seeing the color affect your perceptions of the stone?

Understanding the gemstone qualities in terms of color is a good starting place. However, this perspective can be incomplete by itself. We were given guidance to try some other perspectives, the next of which is sound.

Perspective 2: Sound

Sound, as well as color, can express qualities on the physical, emotional, mental, and spiritual levels. It takes practice to become sensitive to sound within your body. However, once you are more intuitively sensitive to sound, it becomes another medium through which you can better understand the properties of gemstones. Sound is also a powerful tool for healing.

Toning is the practice of making sounds with your voice for healing. To label particular tones, you can use a pitch pipe or a musical instrument. To loosen up your voice and get acquainted with making sounds and tones, try the following exercises:

1. This first clearing exercise can be done anywhere and is good for the release of physical and emotional tension. Begin as low as you can go and make a sound like a siren, which moves up the scale as high as you can go, and back down again. Do this several times and notice the reaction in your body. Do you feel al little lighter and freer?

2. Try making different tones and sounds and see which ones you like and which tones resonate or reverberate inside you. You might find yourself sighing, grunting, focusing on one tone, or making up a little tune. Notice whether your body feels more charged. You are making an intuitive connection with sound.

Another tool that we found helpful in learning how to work with sound, is a set of tuning forks. The vibrations from a tuning fork give a stronger, more focused energy than the more diffuse vibrations of the voice. They are well worth the expense, if you are interested in further exploring sound and gemstones. To activate a tuning fork, strike it against something hard, such as a scrap of wood, and hold it as close as possible to the stone or your body.

In order to create a way of thinking about sound, we aligned the tones with color, using the following resonances:

Red	C	Pink	F#
Red-orange	C#	Turquoise	G
Orange	D	Blue	G#
Yellow-orange	D#	Indigo	A
Yellow	E	Lavender	A#
Green	F	Violet, magenta	B

Using a system such as this can be a useful way of organizing your perceptions; however, we have seen other resonances between color and sound that work effectively for their creators. By paying attention to your perceptions, you will learn what resonances work best for you.

We now introduce the idea of a "dominant frequency" that we have called the "soul tone." _Everything in Nature has a dominant frequency or soul tone that expresses spiritual qualities that are related to its highest purpose._ This tone expresses a _relationship_ between you and the gemstone. For this reason, the tone will vary from person to person, because it reflects your beliefs and perceptions concerning the gemstone. We first discovered this as we noticed that Jonathan and I sometimes disagreed on the soul tone. We have come to understand that each of us habitually tunes into slightly different frequency levels, and so a half tone lower or higher becomes more effective.

Use the tones that we have given as starting points. The right tone will feel like a yes, or an increased energetic charge. Your body may drink it in, or you may feel other signs of heat or stimulation.

Experiment with the given tone, and also with the half and whole tones on either side of it. If none of these tones work, it most likely means that the stone has a different meaning or function for you, and you will need to find the resonating tone. Using the soul tone enhances the emotional, mental, and spiritual effects of the gemstone.

We determined the tones by placing the stone on a clear quartz crystal cluster for amplification. Then we used a tuning fork to find the dominant frequency by holding the vibrating fork to the stone and asking, "Is this the soul tone?"

We give our perceptions on soul tones in the discussion of the individual stones. Some stones, such as clear quartz crystal, seem to resonate to more than one tone, probably because they affect a wider range of frequencies.

Also, the composition of the stone affects the soul tone. For example, chrysocolla is often found intergrown with quartz, malachite, and turquoise, so its soul tone can vary within the range of a whole tone.

You can also clear and charge a stone with its soul tone. To do this, sound the tone, and focus your awareness on the stone being charged. You will need to keep toning until you sense that the stone is charged. This process can take a while, particularly with stones that you have used on the body. With practice and patience you can learn to discriminate how the sounds affect your gemstones.

Your beliefs will affect your intuitive perceptions. Therefore, it is useful to keep records of your discoveries in order to compile data to help you understand your perceptions. As our own discrimination has become more finely tuned, we have changed our perceptions of some of the soul tones. We expect to do so again, because we know that this is an evolving process.

The Rutilated Quartz Deva closes with this explanation of the healing process with sound:

Each part of your being creates its own sound that indicates a normal flow of life-force energies. When I sense discordant vibrations coming from an area, I lock into the frequency that takes me directly to the areas needing my essence. I then help to restore the normal sound. You have the capacity to be a most infinitely beautiful symphony.

Perspective 3: Chakra and Subtle Body Affinities

We have described in Chapter 2 how the aura consists of layers, or subtle bodies. In our system we refer to three subtle bodies. It is most comfortable to work with the etheric subtle body, which is about 1/4 inch to 2 or 3 inches above the physical body. Stones placed on the body directly affect the etheric level. We sense the emotional and mental subtle bodies to be from 3 to 4 inches to about a foot above the physical body. The spiritual subtle body (or bodies) extends from about a foot to 2 or 3 feet from the physical body.

Although a stone can affect all of the subtle bodies, each stone has a particular affinity with one or more subtle bodies and one or more chakras. These affinities are related to their spiritual purpose. When you hold a stone, it will work most strongly with the subtle body or bodies where it has an affinity, and you may feel its energy in different ways. As a hypothetical example, you might notice that physically, your circulation seems speeded up, and mentally and emotionally, you feel more determined to focus on your goals. You might notice a sensation of heat in your right shoulder and solar plexus, where you have carried some fear about moving ahead. The stone is infusing its energy throughout your subtle body system to restore balance.

When you place a stone on a chakra, you will affect the etheric body even more strongly. You will also affect the emotional, mental, and spiritual issues involved at that chakra. Placing stones on various chakras helps to direct life-force energy for balancing in all of the subtle bodies, resulting in a more powerful physical realignment.

The relationship between the chakras and the stones can also help you understand the qualities of stones as they relate to personal issues. We followed the method given below to determine the chakra and subtle body affinities of a stone:

1. It is easiest to work with a partner, but you can also try this on your own.

2. In addition to the gemstone, you will need a large clear quartz crystal that you will hold in your sending hand, and a smaller clear quartz crystal that will be placed on the body. You will also need gem water or a gem essence for each stone, for optimal amplification of the qualities (See Chapter 5).

3. It helps to practice a meditation or breathing technique that aligns your chakras. This is because the chakras that need energy may respond to a stone whether or not they have an affinity with it. With practice, you can learn to tell the difference between a chakra affinity and a chakra that is taking in life-force energy.

4. Put a drop of the gem water on the tip of both crystals.

5. Begin at the root chakra and place the small crystal so that it is pointing toward the stone. Hold the larger crystal in your sending hand with the point toward your fingertips. (If you are working with a partner, they will hold the large crystal in their sending hand.)

6. Rotate your hand-held crystal counterclockwise about 1 or 2 inches above the root chakra at the etheric level and sense the energy. Your receiving hand is held palm up.

7. Next, rotate the crystal about 4 or 5 inches above the root at the emotional and mental level.

8. Finally, rotate the crystal about a foot or more above the body at the spiritual subtle body level. Compare the energy sensations. At the root chakra you can tell which of the subtle bodies the stone will affect most strongly.

9. Place the stone on the lower abdomen chakra and repeat the three rotations. Continue the process until you have checked all the chakras. At one or more chakras you will notice more tingling and a stronger sense of the qualities, as though the chakra has come to life. You may also notice energy sensations at all three subtle body levels.

If you try this and sense very little, repeat the process after you have worked with the stones in your own way. It takes practice to increase your sensitivity.

Our perceptions of chakra and subtle body affinities are given with each stone in Part 2. On page 64 you will find an illustration of chakra locations (Figure 3-1), page 65 includes a summary of the meanings for each chakra (Figure 3-2). At the end of Chapter 7 you will find charts that list the chakra affinities and soul tones of the stones (Figures 7-4, 7-5). You may find over a period of time that your perceptions about chakra affinities change as you continue to receive guidance from the gemstones. As you grow you will work with stones in different ways.

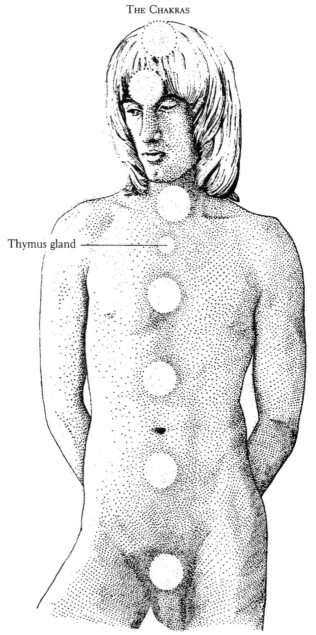

THE CHAKRAS

Thymus gland

FIGURE 3-1. Diagram of the Chakras and Thymus Gland

Figure 3-2. Summary of Chakra Information

CHAKRA	MEANING	LOCATION	AFFIRMATIONS
ROOT	Physical vitality: Basic will to be.	Base of the spine/ pubic bone.	"I honor the natural physical vitality of my body and take care of it wisely." "I AM and the world welcomes me." "I live courageously, taking action to express my being."
LOWER ABDOMEN OR SPLEEN	Connecting with others through your feelings. Assimilating and letting go of our experience.	Midway between navel and pubic bone.	"I assimilate right understanding through my feelings and senses." "I welcome change and freely let go of what I don't need." "I am enough." "I trust the universe to supply my abundance and prosperity."
SOLAR PLEXUS	Developing self-confidence and building personal power.	Two inches above the navel.	"I own my strength and power." "I appreciate all the wonderful qualities that make me unique."
HEART	Developing compassion for all, especially yourself.	Heart.	"I accept myself fully as I am." "I am truly loved."
THROAT	Speaking your truth creatively. Giving service.	Throat.	"I now say what needs to be said." "I value and express my creativity." "My purpose is to serve others with my unique gifts."
THIRD EYE	Regulator and catalyst. Seat of your intuitive knowing.	Brow, midway between and slightly above the eyelashes.	"I now release early and past-life experiences which do not serve my highest good." "I accept responsibility for creating my reality." "My intuitive connection with my Higher Spiritual Nature is expanding and becoming clear."
CROWN	Merging with your basic identity of God/ Goddess/All That Is.	Top of head	"I merge with the unity of all life." "I act in alignment with my Higher Spiritual Nature."

Chapter 4

LEARNING ABOUT GEM ENERGY: THE HEALING PROCESS & THE 4 ELEMENTS

This chapter explains two final perspectives for viewing gemstone energy. Our fourth perspective involves perceiving the functional relationship between gemstones and thoughts and emotions. Jonathan and I believe that healing is a process that involves releasing imbalanced thoughts and feelings, incorporating new beliefs, and expanding into new levels of awareness.

Our fifth perspective involves relating the qualities of a stone to one of the four Elements. This can allow you to develop a way to further describe *how the energy moves and its spiritual qualities.*

Perspective 4: Healing with the 3-step Process

To be human is to experience your essential vulnerability. How do you keep from being swept under the tides of incomprehensible happenings and painful experiences? An age-old solution to this question is having compassion for you and others. The way of compassion takes lifetimes to learn. However, you can turn for help to the Kingdoms of Nature.

You can begin by recognizing that whether or not you acknowledge it, all of us carry pain. When something painful happens to you, you inevitably ask, "Why me?" When you are young you answer this question to the best of your understanding, but often you do not draw the correct conclusion. "Something is wrong with me," "I am basically unlovable," or "It was my fault," are erroneous conclusions that seem to make sense at the time. These false beliefs are empowered by the painful emotions of the experience. Until they are released and resolved, this emotional energy is locked into your physical and subtle bodies, restricting the flow of positive life-force energy on all levels: physical, emotional, mental, and spiritual. If the experience is an extremely painful memory, you may block the memory from your conscious mind and attempt to resolve it by forgetting it. The memory then becomes stored in your subconscious mind, where you may carry it for the rest of your life and into future lifetimes, until it is resolved. This is partly the basis of karma; you create opportunities in this lifetime to resolve the false conclusions of the past.

One of my early past-life regressions helped me understand a prior relationship with a particular man. At the time we shared an interest in pioneer buildings and working with wood, and I depended on him for advice in practical matters. However, there were difficulties in our emotional relationship, and I often wondered why we were drawn together. We both knew that it was a temporary affair. In the regression I discovered that he had been my father in a previous lifetime when we had homesteaded in Tennessee. My mother (his wife) had died when I was 2 or 3. I remember that I was angry with him for never sharing or talking about that grief, and I was estranged from him in that life. In the regression I forgave him and shared the mutual grief with him. Afterward it was as though a cord had been cut. I had a sense of being totally at peace with this relationship and its purpose.

We often draw painful experiences into our present lives that are based on beliefs such as, "I'm always a victim." Sometimes these experiences are an attempt at resolution, and sometimes they are the perpetuation of a belief that has continued over lifetimes. The keys for resolution are also present in some manner, and you must choose to look for them.

The first step in our three-step model of healing is to clear negative emotions and beliefs. In order to do this you must first become aware of your beliefs. You must be brave enough to allow the painful feelings that empower your beliefs to surface. This can be a difficult process because you are very vulnerable when you express your deepest feelings and can be hurt by a lack of support or acceptance. Often, rather than risking being hurt again, you choose to be silent and try to forget, much to the detriment of your physical and emotional health. It is helpful for you to understand your vulnerability so that you can create the necessary support.

A painful emotion, similar to "dis-ease" in the physical body, is a call for help and attention to an experience that needs resolution and compassion. *Expressing an emotion is actually a release of pain* or blocked energy that often illuminates a particular memory and the negative belief attached to it. For example, when I examined the experience of feeling ignored by a former friend, I discovered that beneath my anger at the friend is grief. That grief came from assuming that the cause of our separation was that there was something wrong with me. After expressing my feelings and releasing some of the blocked emotional energy, I could then see more clearly what I needed to affirm. The combination of new understanding and released tension healed the situation.

The idea that expressing emotions is a sign of weakness has significantly contributed to our lack of well-being. This idea is part of the male belief system in our culture and contributes to a great deal of unnecessary suffering. When we hold feelings inside and try to ignore them, we become more emotionally insensitive, unable to feel and express deep joy, and less able to understand the needs of others.

A key to clearing emotional pain and becoming more aware of your limiting beliefs is compassion and self-acceptance. You often wish to tell your troubles to someone else so that you can receive a bit of Unconditional Love and compassion. We need to encourage each other to listen to the unspoken words of doubt and discouragement, express our emotional pain, and give acceptance and love. You need to encourage yourself to merge with the compassion that is within you. Compassion can be visualized and felt as a friend, a Guardian Angel, a free-spirited child, a spiritual teacher such as Christ, or in any manner you wish. As you continue to ask for compassion and self-acceptance as part of the release process, the emotional pain lessens and experiences can be resolved.

The various Kingdoms of Nature, including the Mineral Kingdom, are another source of compassion and self-acceptance. Each stone is a unique expression of Unconditional Love, and you can experience that Love once you learn to merge with stones on a spiritual level. Depending on how you choose to work with their energies at a given time, stones can help you to release and heal emotional pain.

The process of clearing negative beliefs and emotions can be described in terms of energy flow. *Imbalance can be sensed as blocked energy; the clearing of this blocked energy is a phenomenon of dispersal that results in the restoration of flow.* It is possible to sense which stones are particularly helpful in the clearing and releasing process by noting whether their energy disperses or clears in some manner. These stones help clear a pathway for subsequent building and expansion by working with dense, blocked energy. Be aware of the manner in which the energy of a stone moves in your body and psyche, and see whether you are guided to "let go" in some manner. You can also use a pendulum and ask, "Are you useful in the clearing process of helping me become aware of and release imbalanced patterns?"

It is interesting to note that the function of many medicinal herbs that help you release toxins in different ways is essentially one of clearing. You need only make a conscious effort to ask for help from the Kingdoms of Nature and it is gladly given.

The next step in healing is an *infusing or building process.* This step, which is often integrated with clearing and release, involves building new and positive ways of thinking to replace the incorrect, imbalanced patterns. This can be likened to putting a new record on the record player. *It is necessary not only to express and release emotional energy, but to identify and change the negative beliefs.* Otherwise, it is possible to get stuck in the emotional pain. The building process takes effort and patience because it is easier to think and act in the old ways. Working with written and spoken affirmations is one of the best ways to build new confidence. Building is also an expansion process in which you go beyond your limitations and travel in new territory, doing things that you might not have dreamed possible earlier.

Once again, *compassion* and *self-acceptance* are key elements. Compassion for yourself and others gives you patience, because building is a step-by-step process. Sometimes, with our increased technology, we want immediate growth and admire people who can do things quickly. All the Kingdoms of Nature teach you that growth is gradual. You need to cultivate persistence and determination as well as delight in being in the moment. Once again, you must accept yourself as you are. The unique healing qualities of stones can be your spiritual building blocks, just as their physical forms give you additional vitality.

In terms of energy movement, building stones infuse and expand, rather than disperse. There can be a sense of heightened well-being on all levels, a stepping-up of physical energies, or an increased appreciation of your unique individuality. This movement is more like a coming together and elevating, rather than a dispersal of blocked energy. Many stones assist in both clearing and building, depending on how you work with their energies. This is particularly true of the stones that have an affinity with the third eye. However, they normally either clear or build more strongly, particularly in combination with certain other stones. In this life you are learning to affirm and express your unique purpose and service. Just as each stone expresses its individual beauty, you can express your unique "colors" with patience and enjoyment.

The third step after clearing and building is *spiritual expansion.* We describe these steps sequentially in order to make them easier to understand, but in reality they are interwoven. In releasing imbalances and building new thought patterns, you emphasize your own individuality and service. *Spiritually expansive energy lifts you out of your mind, emotions, and physical body and into a Unity with All Life.* As you merge with the Infinite Consciousness, you expand beyond rational knowledge. Every stone can teach you about spiritual expansion because they are innately connected with Unconditional Love and Light. However, certain stones, such as clear quartz crystal, are bridges in helping you understand that your own Goodness is part of the larger beauty of All That Is. The energy from these stones is very light, more finely tuned, and sometimes more difficult to describe. *It is a building energy that works at higher levels of spiritual awareness.*

We can illustrate the concept of the three-step healing process with a frequency band. This is like a color spectrum, with the densest energy on the left and the higher frequencies on the right. There are no sharp delineations in this band. Instead, the band illustrates a gradual flow of energies from left to right.

Clearing	Building and Infusing	Spiritual Expansion

Figure 4-1. The Frequency Band

Stones have specialties according to whether they help you disperse dense imbalanced energy, build balanced energy, or move into higher frequencies of energy.

Integrated with your growth process of clearing, building, and spiritually expanding your understanding is the need for *grounding*. During times of change it can be helpful to focus on what supports and roots you. This may be a familiar routine or a special place to which you keep returning. That which grounds you is like a *core of balance* from which you release or expand.

Stones can serve as grounders or stabilizers because of their dense physical form and their function as a foundation for physical life. Certain stones play an important role in helping you integrate your awareness, honor your physical body, and focus on the daily tasks of living.

Perspective 5: The 4 Elements of Nature

In working with stones, it can be helpful to relate their qualities to the energies of the four Elements. To illustrate this I will give a practical example from my life. We were making regular visits to a small town park where part of the walking path wound along a creek. I would listen to the sound of the water and imagine it flowing through me, carrying away with it various frustrations and thoughts that I wished to release. Having worked with water in this way I can now *feel* it flowing through me with all its cooling, fluid qualities. I am aware of what kinds of thoughts occur to me. Sometimes it is the idea that things are always changing. This thought sometimes occurs to me when I feel stuck. Sometimes I cry and feel the water as part of my tears, and I become particularly aware of this movement. The flowing water itself seems to be affirming my release and acknowledgment of pain. Sometimes the water seems very healing, as though it is a liquid lotion bathing me with loving hands. At other times I feel soothed and still. My relationship with water continues to change, and as I open to its qualities, I am able to receive what I need.

You can relate to any Element of Nature's Kingdoms in this way. The perceptions you receive relate to your own beliefs, your own intuitive language, and what you need at any given time. The Elements heal on all levels because they are essential forms of life-force energy.

On the physical level, you receive Earth energy from the foods you eat. This helps build the form of your physical body. For this reason it is important to eat natural, unprocessed foods so that you receive the maximum amount of life-force energy. Water is used externally for cleansing. herbal baths and swimming revitalize the etheric energy field. Your body is made up of more than 70 percent water. Water taken internally, in the form of herbal teas, for example, also strengthens the energy fields.

Anyone who has practiced deep breathing as part of a transformational discipline knows the revitalizing effects of the air we breathe. *Prana* is a Sanskrit term for breath and "life-force energy." *Pranayama,* or regulated yogic breathing, is considered to be a gateway to expanded consciousness on all levels.

Sunlight (Fire on the physical level) is a source of vitamin D essential to human health.

On the emotional and mental levels it is helpful to think of the Elements as *movements* of energy that instill qualities associated with their movement. As you visualize the Elements, notice how the energy moves in your body. Just as I worked with the creek water, you can work with the movement of any Element. The next time you are out on a windy day, find out from which direction the wind is blowing. Then experiment with different types of thoughts and find which feel most comfortable to you. For example, we found that winds that come from the North or West are particularly good for releasing thoughts and purifying your being. When you stand in winds from the South and East you can affirm new growth and expansion.

Several years ago as we walked on a nearby frozen lake, we discovered that ice is very helpful in clearing thoughts. As we stood, we focused on a difficult situation and concentrated on releasing our imbalanced thoughts until our minds were clear and the pain was gone. Ice seems to disperse energy quickly and intensely, possibly because of the density of the water. After we stepped off the ice and were back in the woods, we were aware of the contrast between the clearing intensity of the ice and the stability of the Earth.

Snow also disperses energy, but in a gentler manner. Its physical whiteness and stillness seem to work well with thoughts of emptying the mind and purifying the energy system.

The Elements can spiritually teach you about your larger purpose in life. By merging with each Element, you can affirm being in harmony with Nature. By noticing which Element seems most meaningful to you, you can receive guidance about the direction to take in your growth.

From the Earth Element, you learn to accept the sacred responsibility that you have as a steward for our precious Earth.

You learn how to properly and continuously align your energies with the Earth so that you can maintain a centeredness and balance as you follow your path. As with all the Elements, you come to appreciate the beauty and perfection of the smallest forms of life you see on the Earth. *Earth qualities are deepening, centering, focusing, and stabilizing.*

By merging with the Water Element you can perceive ways to integrate your sensitivity through the use of the emotional body. You can let go of conditional responses to life experiences and move toward Unconditional Love and greater acceptance of yourself and others. You understand the aspect of feeling that exists beyond the physical level and allows a true expansion of your senses to occur. *Water qualities are flowing, surrendering, harmonizing, and accepting.*

By merging with Air you learn how to be spiritually mindful and how to utilize the energies of the mind for the highest good of all concerned. You move from a space of "me-ness" to one of encompassing the infinite totality of All That Is. *Air energies are emptying and uplifting.*

By merging with Fire you learn a purposeful focus of the life-force energy. On the Earth Plane it is sometimes referred to as power. What you learn is how to take a concept and give it greater clarity and discernment through proper utilization of your mind and will. *Fire qualities are purifying, stimulating, expansive, and action-oriented.*

The Elements of Earth, Water, Air, and Fire (Sun) are necessary for your physical life on this Planet. You must learn that their spiritual qualities are necessary for your spiritual life as well.

Part 2

THE INDIVIDUAL GEMSTONES

I n Part 1 we acquainted ourselves with the Mineral Kingdom and reviewed five perspectives that can give insight into the spiritual qualities and purposes of the stones. Now that your perceptual tools have been sharpened, you are ready to know the individual stones. Meeting a stone is like making a friend. The true depth and beauty of a friend is revealed through the shared experience of struggles as well as the simple pleasures of life. These friends have much to give if you ask them to share with you.

When you meet a friend you may first notice their outer appearance, and ask where they live. So, first we give you the *physical aspects* of the stone. Then we listen to the innermost essence of the stone in the *Devic channeling*. When you are attuning yourself to the spiritual qualities of a stone, you are attuning to the Deva of that stone. The Consciousness of every mineral is linked to an interconnected Higher Order of Beings, so that when you are connected with an individual Deva, you have access to many levels of wisdom and understanding. The Deva explains the spiritual qualities and purpose of the stone.

We then share with you our own perceptions of the perspectives given in Part 1. The section on *spiritual aspects* contains the soul tone, the chakra and subtle body affinities, an energy focus for healing, and a descriptive Element. Note that in the chakra affinities *1* indicates a primary affinity and *2* indicates a secondary affinity. The different perspectives, as well as the Devic channeling, provide clues about ways to relate the stones to your everyday life, which we describe in the section on *co-creating with the gemstone*. Co-creating refers to wearing the stone, holding it, placing it on the body, meditating with it, or taking in its essence. A *gem essence* is an infusion of the gem's energies in pure water and alcohol, for the purpose of internal consumption. (In Part 3, Chapter 6, you will find a discussion of how to make and utilize gem essences.) Finally we end with an *affirmation* for each gemstone that captures the essence of its purpose.

Certain stones such as galena, pyrite, and rutilated quartz have a more generalized or broadly focused energy than other minerals. This broadly focused energy makes these stones more versatile in their use. In this respect they are like the metals copper, gold, and silver, which are described at the end of Part 2. The metals are also more broadly focused and versatile in their use, which makes them ideal partners with other stones in jewelry.

To get to know your stones, it helps to become familiar with them through your own intuitive process. Use this part of the book as another viewpoint or reference, rather than the definitive word on a particular stone. Let us now meet some new friends.

Chapter 5

INDIVIDUAL GEMSTONES AND METALLIC ELEMENTS

The Gemstones

Alexanderite

Physical Aspects

The name "alexanderite" refers to a variety of chrysoberyl, usually green, that appears red, purplish, or purplish violet under artificial light. The most common colors of chrysoberyl are golden yellow, greenish yellow, and golden brown. These are called simply chrysoberyl.

Alexanderite was first discovered in the Ural mountains of Russia in the 1830s and named for Czar Alexander. The best gem quality alexanderite now comes from Brazil, Sri Lanka, and Rhodesia, as well as other locations including the United States.

Alexanderite is a hard stone (8 1/2) and belongs to the orthorhombic system with its long prismatic crystals. It is often found with beryl and tourmaline in granite pegmatites.

The Alexanderite Deva

I heighten your awareness of the spiritual energy that is available to you in the present moment. This awareness strengthens your sense of self, opening you to new possibilities. As you spend time with me, you are learning to fully comprehend the gifts of Spirit that you have brought with you, which are catalysts for your personal healing.

When you experience pain and suffering you conclude that Spirit is abandoning you, and you may experience anger, bitterness, regret, and feelings of loss and isolation. I strengthen your connection to Spirit in the present moment in a way that neutralizes or rebalances this thought pattern. Over a period of time, you will have fewer tendencies to react to life as you have in the past.

Being with my energy allows you to move forward toward who you are becoming. It is necessary to trust this process of change and transformation that is unfolding, and to open to the flow of Unconditional Love within.

Spiritual Aspects

Soul Tone: A#

Chakra Affinities: Third Eye

Subtle Body Affinities: Mental, Spiritual

Energy Focus: Spiritual Expansion

Element: Air

Cocreating with Alexanderite

Alexanderite impacts energetically on more subtle levels with the longer-term issues of coming to terms with suffering and reestablishing a connection with Spirit. It seems to work by heightening your awareness and sensitivity to the spiritual energy available to you in the present moment. By allowing this energy to move through you, the negative impact of feeling separated from Spirit is neutralized, and you may feel more detached from the influence of past pain.

Alexanderite does not seem to bring into your awareness more specific conscious understandings, unlike some other stones such as lapis lazuli. Release expectations about what insights you might gain, and work with it over a period of time as a catalyst for spiritual transformation. It creates an energy space of greater Unconditional Love that allows change to happen.

Affirmation

"I OPEN TO THE GREATER POSSIBILITIES THAT CHANGE IS BRINGING IN MY SPIRITUAL GROWTH."

Amazonite

Physical Aspects

Amazonite, or amazon stone, as it is sometimes called, is an opaque, blue-green potassium feldspar. Its chemical composition is potassium aluminum silicate. It has a hardness of 6–6 1/2 and a triclinic crystalline structure. In the United States there are deposits in Colorado, Pennsylvania, and Virginia. Amazonite is also found in Russia, Brazil, Malagasy Republic, and India. It is usually cut in cabochon or round for bead necklaces.

The Amazonite Deva

I provide a sense of continuity and understanding between the world of the body and the world of the spirit. Through my energies you may experience hope, joy, and transcendence. I can help you give meaning and value to your life regardless of what you have chosen to do, so that your transitions are more peaceful.

Did you know that all lifestreams enter the Earth plane with the highest ideals of what they seek to do? I speak to those of you who have come a long way in space and time to be here on the Earth plane, and to those of you who contemplate a premature exit from the physical vehicle. Sometimes you may feel a sense of disillusionment, and perhaps even seek to leave the Earth plane, because you feel you have accomplished nothing.

I help you to bless what you have done, rather than mourn what the goal was to have been.

To all of you I say that through spiritual expansion, you will come to know and understand the limitlessness of your being and how truly multifaceted you are. Your relationship to life itself undergoes a transformation and you see that you are part of Infinity, connected with All That Is. Your sense of spiritual compassion and understanding increases as you witness numerous paths that lead to total Unity with All. Your task is to make this Earth a heaven, and to heal that which is of Earth, so that what you seek will already be with you.

Spiritual Aspects

Soul Tone: A, A#. Most of our stones test A.

Chakra Affinities: Third Eye (1), Thymus Gland (l), Crown (2)*

Subtle Body Affinities: Spiritual (Affects all subtle bodies on the Thymus Gland.)

Energy Focus: Spiritual Expansion

Element: Air

Cocreating with Amazonite

Amazonite can be held in meditation to lift you beyond your personal self and help you merge with spirit. If you fear out-of-body experiences, amazonite can calm this fear. If you know of someone who is terminally ill, that person can benefit from having the energies of amazonite in his or her presence.

Note: (1) indicates primary affinity, (2) indicates secondary affinity.

Affirmation

"I AM PROTECTED BY THE LIGHT AS I MOVE THROUGH TRANSITIONS IN MY LIFE, AND I BLESS WHAT I HAVE ACCOMPLISHED."

Amber

Physical Aspects

Amber is organic in origin, consisting of the fossilized resin of the pine tree, *Pinus succinifera*. It was formed during the Eocene period 50 to 70 million years ago. It has a hardness of 2 1/2 and an amorphous crystalline structure. In color, amber most commonly ranges from light yellow and gold to brown and red. It often has inclusions of insects and parts of plants. There are large reserves of amber along the shores of the Baltic Sea, where it can be picked up on the beaches and in shallow water after heavy storms. There is also a well-known deposit in Poland, some minor deposits along the Atlantic coast in the United States, and in the Dominican Republic.

The Amber Deva

I teach you that physical vitality is maintained through a lightness of spirit. Sometimes you seek instantaneous results and then you become weighed down with a sense that the growth process will take forever. I help you elevate your thoughts to a different level, where you can see the meaning in what is taking place without judging the time and effort involved. Although it is not my only function, I encourage laughter. Laughter frees heavy energy so that you breathe more freely and lightly. You are continually evolving at different stages in your soul's development. Some aspects are accelerating more rapidly than other aspects. Be patient with who you are right now and accept yourself without judgment. Doing this will give you a sunny, light disposition that can see the humor in things.

Spiritual Aspects

Soul Tone: C

Chakra Affinities: Root (1), Lower Abdomen (1), Solar Plexus (1)

Subtle Body Affinities: Etheric, Emotional/Mental, Spiritual

Energy Focus: Building

Element: Air

Cocreating with Amber

When you feel that life is a burden or a struggle, or you feel weighted down with responsibility, amber with its uplifting energies teaches you to walk lightly. It can help you see life with more humor and to find the joy in each step of the way. Amber can create a happy balance between the affairs of daily living and the movement toward higher mental and spiritual expansion.

Affirmation

"I BUILD MY PHYSICAL VITALITY THROUGH LIGHTNESS OF SPIRIT."

Amethyst

Physical Aspects

Amethyst is a member of the quartz family, a silicon dioxide with a hardness of 7 and a trigonal crystalline structure. In its crystalline form amethyst ranges from pale to deep violet. Its color is thought to be due to minute traces of iron. Amethyst quartz is a rougher, more compact form of amethyst that is striped with milky quartz and often polished. Some amethysts can lose their color in daylight but the original color can be restored by X-ray radiation. Amethysts are often found in geodes in alluvial deposits. A geode is a nodule of siliceous volcanic rock containing quartz crystals or quartz agate inside. The most important deposits of amethyst are in Brazil, Uruguay, and the Malagasy Republic.

The Amethyst Deva

My purpose is to heighten your spiritual awareness and to help you remember the Divinity that is you.

Self is viewed from a higher spiritual perspective. Letting go of your old ways of thinking about self and others, and becoming One with your Divine Essence, transforms the you that was into the you that is. The process of transition, whether in the physical body at death, or in your mind during the growth process, is merely a change in your level of awareness that can bring you greater self-fulfillment. My transformation of your energies is truly a purification and a cleansing, and with my peace, you need not fear death in any form.

Spiritual Aspects

Soul Tone: B

Chakra Affinities: Crown (1), Thymus Gland (1), Third Eye (2)

Subtle Body Affinities: Spiritual, Etheric, Emotional/Mental

Energy Focus: Clearing

Element: Air

Cocreating with Amethyst

With its purifying energies, amethyst helps clear and transform energies in the environment where it is placed. Therefore, it is an aid to help you release imbalanced energies during the day, or protect yourself in an imbalanced environment. Amethyst has a calming effect that helps you release unnecessary thoughts. The sense is one of being purified and freed of burdens. Holding an amethyst or taking its essence can be a way of preparing yourself for spiritual work. Amethyst can also be used to help you understand your dreams. Because it works mainly with the spiritual body, it can be helpful in utilizing other stones or practices in conjunction with amethyst specifically to affect your conscious mind, emotions, or physical body. What it does is to provide a "light space" where you can get your bearings. Amethyst can help you remember that you are more than the principal actor or actress in your life drama. You are indeed the Light.

Affirmation

"I RELEASE ALL NEED FOR SELF-IDENTITY."

Apatite

Physical Aspects

Apatite is the most common of all phosphorus-bearing minerals, and is widely used in the manufacture of phosphate fertilizers. The name derives from the Greek word "apate" meaning "deceit" because it is similar in appearance to aquamarine, olivine, and fluorite.

Although it is mined in a variety of colors, we have seen the yellow shades most frequently. Its crystalline structure is hexagonal, with a hardness of 5 and a greasy luster. Apatite is mined for its beauty in Germany, Spain, Brazil, Mexico, Canada, and the United States. Our perceptions are based on the yellow apatite crystals.

The Apatite Deva

You have a responsibility to ensure that your actions do not adversely affect the quality of life of any other physical form, human or otherwise. I work with the area of forethought, encouraging you to take the time to think about the impact of your actions before you initiate them. Spontaneity flows from a harmonious sense of the entire picture. Impulsivity can flow from a vacuum where you have isolated yourself from the effects of your actions, in favor of a more immediate gratification.

Acting without foresight is a selfishness that often originates with a lack of self-worth. I act as a mental illuminator, to bring you more awareness of the Light within you. Through my energies I initiate a reprogramming of the mind so that you can understand the wholeness of who you are. Once you connect with your Inner Light, self-judgment will diminish and be replaced by Unconditional Love for self.

As the energies of Planet Earth undergo change, my role in the evolution of human consciousness will become more pronounced. Self must be seen as a cell that is part of the whole, where foresight and thought result in right action. This is not only the natural way to be, it is the only way to be.

Spiritual Aspects

Soul Tone: E

Chakra Affinities: Solar Plexus

Subtle Body Affinities: Mental/Emotional

Energy Focus: Building

Element: Air

Cocreating with Apatite

Apatite encourages you to take action at the appropriate time. When you are prone to acting out of your emotions or acting impulsively without thinking, apatite tells you to slow down and consider where your greatest power lies. Rather than reacting with desire or anxiety about the future, apatite assists you into the driver's seat, where you can better choose both the timeliness and harmony of your actions with your Highest Good.

The energies of apatite combine well with black tourmalinated quartz, orange carnelian, jade, aquamarine, clear kunzite, yellow fluorite, and clear quartz.

Affirmation

"I ACT WITH FORESIGHT, IN HARMONY WITH ALL THAT IS."

Aquamarine

Physical Aspects

Aquamarine, like emerald, is a member of the beryl family. It is named for the resemblance of its color to seawater. Aquamarine is an aluminum beryllium silicate that gets its color from traces of iron. It has a hardness of 71/2–8 and a trigonal crystalline structure. Rough aquamarine crystals are fairly common and they have a striated appearance, somewhat like tourmaline. Lighter aquamarine is sometimes heated to change it to a darker blue. Aquamarine is found in the pegmatites and coarse granites of Brazil, Malagasy Republic, the United States, as well as numerous other locations.

The Aquamarine Deva

I encourage you to perceive your daily service as a way to care for others and grow spiritually. When you feel in conflict about whether what you are doing has meaning, I can help you understand how you are fulfilling the spiritual purpose in your life. My energies give a sense of continuity that can reassure you when you are discouraged about whether or not you are accomplishing what you have set out to do. I tell you to trust that what you share with others in your daily service has value and meaning, especially when you see your work as a way of giving Unconditional Love to others.

Spiritual Aspects

Soul Tone: G, F#. Darker aquamarines test F#. Pale light aquamarines test G.

Chakra Affinities: Throat (1), Heart (2)

Subtle Body Affinities: Emotional/Mental, Spiritual, Etheric

Energy Focus: Building

Element: Water

Cocreating with Aquamarine

When you are feeling discouraged or your work feels empty, aquamarine can help you find deeper satisfaction and healing in your daily work. Aquamarine teaches you to value yourself and what you give to others. It expands a limited view of the results of your efforts. The essence is both reassuring and uplifting, because it helps you find spiritual fulfillment in everything you do.

Affirmation

"I AM REASSURED AND UPLIFTED BY THE KNOWLEDGE THAT MY WORK IS MY LOVE MADE VISIBLE." (INSPIRED BY KAHLIL GIBRAN)

Aventurine

Physical Aspects

Aventurine is a green microcrystalline quartz with white and sparkly inclusions of hematite or mica that give a spangled appearance. As with other members of the quartz family, it is silicon dioxide, with a hardness of 7 and a trigonal crystalline structure. It is most often found in India, Brazil, and Russia.

The Aventurine Deva

My energies encourage you to move from a limited vision of your capabilities to a more diverse exploration of your creative gifts. From the moment you decide to incarnate in a physical

vehicle on Planet Earth, the process of exploring your personal reality begins. Do you seek experiences that are going to support a narrowly focused state of being or do you desire to embrace the broader facets of life? Sometimes you may be unaware of gifts and interests that you possess, and sometimes you stubbornly refuse to explore those gifts of which you are already aware. In order to truly understand and fulfill your spiritual purpose you must explore the possibilities. I can calm the apprehension and uncertainty that is behind a limited focus of what you can express. I build your self-worth by encouraging you to experience alternative ways of being in your world.

Spiritual Aspects

Soul Tone: E

Chakra Affinities: Solar Plexus (1), Lower Abdomen (1), Heart (2)

Subtle Body Affinities: Emotional/Mental, Spiritual, Etheric

Energy Focus: Building

Element: Water

Cocreating with Aventurine

Aventurine has a gentle, flowing expansiveness that helps you see that you can do more things than you thought you could do. It encourages exploration and creating in new ways. Aventurine could be helpful in career assessment and during transitions from functioning in one role to being called upon to act in new ways.

Affirmation

"I EXPAND MY VISION OF WHO I CAN BE."

Azurite

Physical Aspects

Azurite is a basic copper carbonate with five percent water and a hardness of 3 1/2–4. It belongs to the monoclinic system. As a secondary copper mineral it is often found with malachite and mined in copper deposits. It takes the form of a dense aggregate, small crystals, or spherical aggregate balls. The most well-known deposits are in the Urals in Russia, Australia, and in this country, in Arizona and Pennsylvania.

The Azurite Deva

As I prepare the way for the Light through denser energy, my energies are those of change and purification. I help you to know and reprogram your subconscious mind so that your intuitive sensitivity is increased. I help you prepare for change through gradual adjustment so that there is a sense of safety and reassurance. In this way I also help you build your spiritual awareness beyond your five senses.

There is another related purpose that I serve. When a soul has been out of a physical vehicle for some time and has decided to reenter the Earth Plane, my energies are infused into the subconscious memory of the being to help alleviate the stress of moving into a denser environment.

I can help you adjust your energies in a balanced manner from denser to finer levels of reality. I give both reassurance and a calm readiness.

Spiritual Aspects

Soul Tone: G#, Stones containing other minerals besides azurite may test G.

Chakra Affinities: Third Eye (1)

Subtle Body Affinities: Emotional/Mental, Spiritual, Etheric

Energy Focus: Clearing

Element: Water/Earth

Cocreating with Azurite

With its steady, deep, inward focus azurite is helpful for past-life work or for reprogramming your subconscious. It is a good stone for meditation because it will help clear and balance your third eye so that it can receive finer energies.

Affirmation

"I FIND PEACE AS I RELEASE EMOTIONAL TIES FROM THE PAST."

Bloodstone

Physical Aspects

Bloodstone, or heliotrope, as it is sometimes called, is an opaque, dark green chalcedony quartz with red spots of jasper. As a member of the quartz family it is silicon dioxide, with a trigonal crystal system and a hardness of 7. The most important deposits are in India, Australia, Brazil, China, and the United States

The Bloodstone Deva

When your will is aligned with your spiritual purpose, I can affirm your perseverance in riding the waves that surface along the path. My energies can assist you in realigning with your spiritual purpose through clearing self-doubts caused by recent memories from present or past lives. Sometimes when there are things in your life that are inconsistent with where you want to be, you simply need to go further in the process toward continuity and balance. Inner power is built through steadily overcoming doubt and fear, and reaffirming what you came to do and learn in this life.

Spiritual Aspects

Soul Tone: C# or C. A bloodstone with more red will resonate to C. Stones that are mostly green resonate at C#.

Chakra Affinities: Root (1), Lower Abdomen (1), Solar Plexus (2)

Subtle Body Affinities: Emotional/Mental, Etheric, Spiritual

Energy Focus: Clearing

Element: Earth/Fire

Cocreating with Bloodstone

Bloodstone can give powerful strength and stamina during a seemingly endless period of difficulty, when there has been despair or loss of hope. Bloodstone helps you see a situation as a challenge and can aid you in clearing feelings of weakness or discouragement.

You can utilize the stone to clear self-doubts that are a result of present- or past-life experiences. First, place bloodstone on the area of the body where blockage is experienced. Second, place a clear quartz crystal with bloodstone essence on the third eye, to facilitate memory, understanding, and release of the experience.

Bloodstone also has the capacity to clear scattered thoughts as you prepare to meditate.

Affirmation

"I AFFIRM THE POWER OF MY PERSEVERANCE TO SEE ME THROUGH ALL SITUATIONS."

Blue Lace Agate

Physical Aspects

Blue lace agate is a light blue, banded microcrystalline quartz, with a hardness of 7. Like other members Of the quartz family it is composed of silicon dioxide and belongs to the trigonal crystal system. The most well-known agate deposits are in southern Brazil and northern Uruguay.

The Blue Lace Agate Deva

Love needs to be the foundation of expression not only to your fellow humans, but to yourself as well. I urge you to speak honestly to yourself, yet without judgment. Whenever you speak in a positive, non-judgmental manner to yourself, this process opens the channel of sharing that can occur between you and other lifestreams. For example, having the spiritual gift of sensitivity means that you may experience things more deeply than other beings. How do you express this spiritual gift? Do you speak of the hardships that sensitivity occasionally brings with it into your life? Or do you speak of the opportunities that open, in order to be a healing catalyst for other lifestreams? Every action that you take in life is a reflection of your growth on your spiritual path. Be sure that what you speak is for your highest purpose and the highest purpose of the other. When this is done, you can be sure that what you say will reach that being where it is most needed at the present moment.

Spiritual Aspects
Soul Tone: G#
Chakra Affinities: Throat (1)
Subtle Body Affinities: Mental, Spiritual
Energy Focus: Building
Element: Earth

Cocreating with Blue Lace Agate
Blue lace agate strengthens a sense of calm centeredness that can help in social situations if you are inclined to draw attention to yourself through your speech. It encourages focus, discernment, and tact in speech, and discourages nervous habits of impulsive chatter or wandering speech. Blue lace agate would be a useful essence for building confidence in public speaking or in general social situations.

Affirmation
"I REFLECT CALM INNER CERTAINTY, AS I SPEAK WITH NON-JUDGMENT AND DISCERNMENT."

Calcite

Physical Aspects

Calcite is a calcium carbonate that comes in a variety of colors including red, green-blue, brown, and black. The clear variety is called Icelandic Spar. Calcite is soft as minerals go, with a Mohs' hardness of 3, so it is not generally used in jewelry. Similar to quartz, it belongs to the trigonal system, and because of its perfect rhombohedral cleavage, it is often sold in the rhombohedral shape. Calcite is the most common of all calcium carbonate minerals and is found in a variety of environments. Calcite is the main constituent of stalagmites and stalactites in limestone caverns. These are formed when water containing carbon dioxide in solution filters through limestone joints, where it evaporates and crystallizes in the shape of columns. Marble is a crystalline limestone consisting of calcite and dolomite in massive form.

We will discuss green, blue, and honey calcite.

The Green Calcite Deva

I work in a cool, gentle, calming manner to ease the reverberations of shock or an overly volatile approach in some aspect of your life. I give you a peaceful sense of being in control of your experiences as well as a sense of safety and reassurance. I can help you bring your feelings into a more relaxed and central place so that you can clear what you need to with a minimum of discomfort. You may feel a lifting of burdens, each time you work with my energies. Those of you who are highly sensitive and vulnerable can benefit from working with my energies.

Green Calcite—Spiritual Aspects

Soul Tone: D
Chakra Affinities: Lower Abdomen (1), Heart (2)
Subtle Body Affinities: Emotional/Mental, Etheric
Energy Focus: Clearing
Element: Water

Cocreating with Green Calcite

Calcite is one of the clearing stones that balances and calms rather than stimulating or encouraging release. Green calcite essence is wonderful as a physical relaxant, especially if you have a churning stomach. If you are nervous and keyed up with minor emotional upsets, calcite will help you relax and calm down, with its soothing gentle energy. It is easy to imagine drifting in the water with calcite, because it also has a flowing quality.

Green Calcite Affirmation

"I RELEASE NERVOUS TENSION AND FEEL CALM AND RELAXED."

Blue Calcite Deva

Energy levels are being intensified within all life forms, and within Planet Earth herself. Many in the Human Kingdom, particularly those whose emotional, mental, and spiritual bodies are highly sensitive, may experience these active energies in a deep manner. When this occurs you may need to have a way to diffuse this impact on your energy system. That is my function. I help to calm your emotional and mental levels so that you can see clearly what action you may need to take in the experience. Where I sense that you are receiving some special benefit through the intensity of your experiences, my energies may just "take the edge off the intensity," so that its volatile nature is only minutely changed. Know that no lifestream within the Human Kingdom is ever able to experience more intensity of change than the energy system is capable of processing.

Blue Calcite—Spiritual Aspects

Soul Tone: E

Chakra Affinities: Solar Plexus (1)

Subtle Body Affinities: Emotional/Mental, Etheric

Energy Focus: Clearing

Element: Water

Cocreating with Blue Calcite

You can take blue calcite when you feel overwhelmed with the intensity of change in your life. Blue calcite lessens the sense of trauma and helps you move through the changes with more peace.

Blue Calcite Affirmation

"I AFFIRM SAFETY AND PEACE DURING TIMES OF INTENSITY."

Honey Calcite Deva

Whenever you are in an intense period of change and you wonder how you are going to make it through, my energies can give you that "extra lift" to help you rise to the occasion.

Honey Calcite—Spiritual Aspects

Soul Tone: D#

Chakra Affinities: Solar Plexus (1)

Subtle Body Affinities: Emotional/Mental, Etheric

Energy Focus: Clearing, Building

Element: Water

Cocreating with Honey Calcite

Honey calcite is helpful during intense periods of change in creating an optimistic strength. It is an aid when you feel disillusioned, tired, or burdened.

Honey Calcite Affirmation

"I REMAIN OPTIMISTIC DURING TIMES OF INTENSITY."

Carnelian

Physical Aspects

Carnelian, sometimes spelled cornelian, is a member of the microcrystalline quartz family. Therefore it is silicon dioxide, with a hardness of 7 and a trigonal crystalline structure. Carnelian ranges from orange-red to orange-brown and various shades of gold. Many carnelians are agates from Brazil and Uruguay. Sometimes they are colored with ferrous nitrate solution to brighten them and show stripes. Natural carnelian has a cloudy distribution of color. Carnelian also comes from India, where the reddish hues are enhanced by exposure to the sun. We will talk about orange and yellow carnelian.

Orange Carnelian Deva

The quality I share with the Human Kingdom is optimism. Being optimistic about your present learning space allows you to act more spontaneously and less fearfully in the tasks of your daily life. I do not enter your energy field with fiery enthusiasm. Rather, I encourage moderation and tolerance. Find the positive opportunities in each day and appreciate the small gifts that you give to others and to yourself. In this way we can work together in building your self-worth. Know always that all is well.

Orange Carnelian—Spiritual Aspects

Soul Tone: D

Chakra Affinities: Lower Abdomen (1), Solar Plexus (1)

Subtle Body Affinities: Emotional/Mental, Etheric

Energy Focus: Building

Element: Earth

Cocreating with Orange Carnelian

With its cheerful vitality, orange carnelian can help you look on the brighter side of things when you are feeling gloomy or a little despondent. Orange carnelian's optimism can also help with decision-making, if you tend to feel irritated with the idiosyncrasies of others or the little mishaps in life. It stimulates you physically to act in moderation. You can also work with it for past-life exploration when intuitively guided to do so.

Orange Carnelian Affirmation

"I FIND SOMETHING POSITIVE TO ENJOY IN EVERY ASPECT OF MY LIFE."

Yellow Carnelian Deva

Through my energies, your sensitivity to your environment is expanded. I help you to focus your energies into experiences that can have positive effects on your life. Life can truly take on new meaning as you open to the vibrant light quality that can be found within all things.

Yellow Carnelian—Spiritual Aspects

Soul Tone: D#

Chakra Affinities: Solar Plexus (1), Lower Abdomen (2)

Subtle Body Affinities: Emotional/Mental, Etheric

Energy Focus: Building

Element: Earth

Cocreating with Yellow Carnelian

Yellow carnelian has a gentler, more refined vibration than orange carnelian. It continues the process begun by orange carnelian of viewing life more optimistically. Therefore, you might work with its essence after you have worked with orange carnelian. Yellow carnelian reassures you that all is flowing well, so that you can enjoy the process.

Affirmation

"I ENJOY THE GIFTS IN MY EVERYDAY LIFE WITH ALL MY SENSES."

Celestite

Physical Aspects

Celestite, or celestine, as it is sometimes called, is a transparent, bluish-white stone with a hardness of 3 1/2–4. It is a strontium sulphate with an orthorhombic crystalline structure. Celestite is found in sedimentary rock deposits, principally in the United States. Celestite was discovered in the excavating of the Erie Canal in New York, and it has also been found in Ohio, California, and Mexico.

The Celestite Deva

The "sacred space" is that inner place at the very core essence of your being where information is translated into "knowing" prior to its expression. To function as a place where "knowing" in its purest form can exist, the vibratory rate there must be at a level where pure light can be present at all times. My energy essence contains the tonal pattern of this sacred space and helps to clear it by infusing a greater Light into it. Whatever happens in the sacred space determines the degree of openness that is present in the throat and third eye chakras. This in turn affects the state of balance on the physical level in those areas of your being. My work with the Human Kingdom in this capacity is ongoing in its nature, since the process of creation and change is essential to spiritual growth.

Spiritual Aspects
Soul Tone: G

Chakra Affinities: Throat (1), Third Eye (1)

Subtle Body Affinities: Mental, Spiritual, Etheric

Energy Focus: Clearing

Element: Air

Cocreating with Celestite
Celestite clears "left brain chatter" so that you can connect with your Higher Guidance. It aids you in dispersing the memory of an incident that keeps playing like a broken record. Its calming effect relaxes and empties your mind for rest, meditation, or when you need a break from mental concentration. On an ongoing basis, celestite can ease doubts coming from the rational mind when you are evaluating your paranormal experiences. With celestite you can better discern whether your guidance is coming from your desires or your Higher Wisdom.

Affirmation
"MY MIND IS RELAXED AND OPEN TO CONNECT WITH MY HIGHER GUIDANCE."

Chalcedony

Physical Aspects

Chalcedony is a name for the microcrystalline quartz group and is also used to describe a waxy, translucent stone that can be bluish-gray or white. In our work we use a white variety, which we will refer to as chalcedony. As a member of the quartz family, it is silicon dioxide with a trigonal structure and a hardness of 7. Because it is porous it can be dyed, so you may need to check and make sure that you have a natural piece. Chalcedony is widely distributed and is most commonly found in Brazil, India, Uruguay, and the Malagasy Republic.

The Chalcedony Deva

I encourage you to express your emotional needs. When you do that, I can bring you calm and peace. If there has been one element lacking pure expression within the Human Kingdom; it is the expression of feelings. Ongoing spiritual expansion requires emotional openness. This does not mean that you internalize all forms of emotional energies that you are exposed to in your life experience. Instead, you learn to accept what is going to be a catalyst for your spiritual growth.

Spiritual Aspects

Soul Tone: Ranges from D to E, depending on how white it is, E being the tone for the whitest stones.

Chakra Affinities: Solar Plexus (1), Lower Abdomen (1)

Subtle Body Affinities: Emotional/Mental, Etheric

Energy Focus: Clearing

Element: Earth/Water

Cocreating with Chalcedony

Chalcedony asks you to be accountable to your own feelings and to be emotionally honest. Sometimes you may find yourself covering your feelings with a veneer that you have it all together, while simultaneously experiencing a sense of numbness or emotional tension. Chalcedony encourages you to express your feelings and to ask for the support you need.

Its gentle, stimulating energy can help you move through times of sadness and regret.

Affirmation

"I TRUST THE MESSAGES MY FEELINGS ARE GIVING ME AND I SPEAK UP FOR WHAT I NEED."

Charoite

Physical Aspects

Charoite is named after the River Chara in Yakutia, Russia, where it was first found. Its beautiful lilac color is distinctive, and with a hardness of 6 it is suitable for the making of vases and other decorative objects. It appears as a massive fibrous aggregate in metamorphic rock formations.

The Charoite Deva

I resonate with the heart, and I act as bridge between how you perceive yourself on a conscious level, and how you know self from a higher spiritual perspective. You need to move into a positive relationship with where you have been. When you separate yourself from Unconditional Love through self-judgement or regret, I help you to forgive yourself, so that you can accept the choices that you made in your earlier life. When you do this, the process empowers you to live your true self more fully. Know that you no longer need to have a box around you that limits your fullest expression.

You may discover that you dismissed your positive qualities, or perceived them as insignificant in your life, because they were not valued by others. I highlight your positive qualities by bringing them into conscious awareness. I say that it is time to create a new view of yourself with the support of Spirit, which embraces both joy and pain. As you integrate this new awareness, you will open yourself to new vistas of spiritual expansion in your life.

Spiritual Aspects

Soul Tone: A#

Chakra Affinities: Third Eye, Heart

Subtle Body Affinities: Spiritual/Emotional

Energy Focus: Clearing

Element: Air/Water

Cocreating with Charoite

Charoite can help you release the anger, guilt, and regret associated with experiences in your past where you wanted love in some form and did not get it. It can also relieve grief, anger, and fear related to the death of a relationship. Charoite can detach you from your emotional body and assist you in moving to a space beyond pain.

You can use a violet flame meditation with it to release the past so that you can understand the higher purposes that your experiences have served.

Affirmations

"I FORGIVE AND ACCEPT MYSELF."

" I AM FORGIVEN AND ACCEPTED BY SPIRIT."

"I HAVE ALWAYS DONE THE BEST THAT I COULD, GIVEN WHAT I KNEW AT THE TIME."

Chrysocolla

Physical Aspects

Chrysocolla is an opaque, blue-green hydrous copper silicate with a hardness of 2–4. It belongs to the monoclinic crystal system and is often found with azurite and malachite as a byproduct of copper mining. It has the property of sticking to the tongue, which can be a test of identification. Major deposits are in the southwestern United States, Chile, the Ural Mountains in Russia, and Zaire. Chrysocolla often contains varying amounts of malachite and quartz, so it is an aggregate stone. Gem quality chrysocolla is called gem silica and is fairly expensive because it is rare. We have worked with both rough and polished chrysocolla.

The Chrysocolla Deva

I teach you to follow the response that can be felt deeply within the heart, to ensure that you are truly aligned with your spiritual purpose. The greater the resistance that occurs in your heart when you are making choices in life, the more certainty there is that your actions are outside the dimensions of your spiritual purpose. When you find yourself hesitating or feeling uncertain about a particular direction, examine your intentions. Is it truly for the highest good of all concerned to move forward in the particular manner that you are proposing? When there is a sense of flow, continuity, and peace within your being, then you are truly aligned with the energies of your spiritual purpose. I tell you that your heart can be your closest companion and advisor as you choose your life path on the Earth Plane.

Spiritual Aspects

Soul Tone: G, F#, or F, depending on the amount of malachite or quartz in the individual stone. The greener stones vibrate to F, and the bluer stones resonate to F# or G.

Chakra Affinities: Throat (1), Heart (2)

Subtle Body Affinities: Emotional/Mental, Spiritual

Energy Focus: Clearing

Element: Water

Cocreating with Chrysocolla

Chrysocolla provides a reassuring encouragement that helps you move through fear in expressing your spiritual purpose. You can work with it during the process of finding more satisfying work, or beginning a new creative expression. Chrysocolla helps clear links with the past as you move into new areas of service, both in your outer and inner worlds. You may also become more aware of different ways to express yourself creatively in a practical manner.

Affirmation

"I LISTEN TO MY HEART, TO FIND AND AFFIRM MY SPIRITUAL PURPOSE."

Chrysoprase

Physical Aspects

Chrysoprase is an opaque, apple green member of the microcrystalline quartz family. Its color comes from the trace mineral nickel, which is present with the basic silicon dioxide. Similar to other quartz, chrysoprase has a hardness of 7 and a trigonal crystalline structure. Gem quality chrysoprase comes from Australia, California, Oregon, and Brazil. It is sometimes colored artificially.

The Chrysoprase Deva

Commit your energies to completing one process each day. Your small successes and accomplishments are just as significant as your major ones. Look for interrelationships between those things you have done and those in the planning stages. My energies encourage this practice, particularly when you have just completed something and aren't sure what to do next. Keep your conscious mind open to opportunities that may "appear out of the blue." Know that there is always a continuity of flow present between the completion of one stage of growth and the start of a new stage. Be patient with your flow and at peace with your process.

Spiritual Aspects

Soul Tone: D

Chakra Affinities: Solar Plexus (1), Lower Abdomen (1)

Subtle Body Affinities: Emotional/Mental, Etheric, Spiritual

Energy Focus: Building

Element: Earth

Cocreating with Chrysoprase

Chrysoprase can aid you in relieving anxiety and apprehension as you move into the unknown. Its grounding stability gives a sense of continuity that helps you focus on the present moment.

Affirmation

"COMPLETING ONE STEP AT A TIME CONNECTS ME WITH MY INNER
ROOTS AND GIVES ME A SENSE OF CONTINUITY IN MY LIFE."

Citrine

Physical Aspects

Citrine is a yellow quartz. It is a silicon dioxide with a hardness of 7 and a trigonal crystalline structure. Many citrines are heat-treated amethysts or smoky quartzes. Brazilian amethyst turns a lemon yellow at about 900 degrees Fahrenheit, and dark yellow at about 1,000 degrees Fahrenheit. The heat-treated stones have a red tint to them. Natural citrine is a pale yellow and is less common. Large deposits of citrine are mined in Brazil and Madagascar.

The Citrine Deva

Synthesis is a quality that I share with the Human Kingdom. I help you incorporate the input from your logical mind and your intuitive mind into your conscious belief system, so that you feel a sense of clarity and resolve. When you are working with your logical mind, I help you separate what is relevant from what is irrelevant, so that you have the key elements in focus. Unfortunately, your society teaches you to ignore your intuitive mind. By doing so you can throw yourself off balance. I strengthen your intuitive perceptions and help you utilize your information in a way that synthesizes the input from your different sources. When you use both your conscious and intuitive mind you are less likely to stew over a situation, and you will be calmer physically. Ultimately, you will develop a greater peace of mind.

I have one other comment that I wish to make. The Human Kingdom has taken it upon itself to alter the color emanations of the different minerals. Though I cannot change the procedure, I state most directly that I am opposed to all attempts to alter the molecular structure of any minerals. This viewpoint is shared by the other Devas wherever this misapplication of energies is occurring.

Spiritual Aspects

Soul Tone: E

Chakra Affinities: Solar Plexus (1), Third Eye (1)

Subtle Body Affinities: Mental, Spiritual, Etheric

Energy Focus: Building

Element: Air

Cocreating with Citrine

When you are feeling pulled by differing points of view, citrine can help you synthesize your understanding. Citrine can open the way for a unifying perspective that often comes from the intuitive mind. Citrine is helpful on an ongoing basis for mental clarity in communicating ideas to others, writing, and problem-solving.

Affirmation

"I THINK AND COMMUNICATE CLEARLY, SYNTHESIZING INFORMATION FROM ALL LEVELS OF MY BEING."

Coral

Physical Aspects

Coral is one of the organic gem materials, consisting of the calcified skeletons of coral polyps. These polyps are tiny, primitive organisms that eventually attach themselves to previous coral growth and secrete a substance that is similar to calcite. The chemical composition of coral is calcium carbonate with magnesium carbonate and traces of organic substances. Coral has a hardness of 3-4 and a vitreous luster when polished. In the gem trade, red, pink, and white corals are the most favored colors. Coral is sensitive to heat, acids, and hot solutions, and the color can fade when worn. Coral is worked with a saw, knife, and file rather than the standard polishing wheels. There are many imitations made from glass, plastic, and other minerals.

Coral is harvested by dragging nets across seabeds. Unfortunately, this method destroys much of the valuable material. Coral is dredged in the Mediterranean and off the coasts of Italy, Algeria, Sicily, Spain, and Japan. We will discuss the white and red corals.

The White Coral Deva

Infinite paths are available for those in the Human Kingdom to follow in the growth cycle each has chosen. It is only natural to want to make things better for those you feel close to. I am here to help you learn to value the unique being that you are. You no longer need to take it personally when people do not listen to what you are saying. With my energies to balance you, you can ask your Higher Self or the Higher Self of another, whether it is in his/her highest good for you to offer suggestions. I broaden your spiritual understanding by teaching you to forgive yourself and others when something has been shared that has not been for the highest good. Forgiveness is truly the quickest way to heal hurt and misunderstanding.

My energies also strengthen you when you feel you are being told what to do by another. With me you can assimilate those energies that are helpful to you in your growth and release other energies without hurt or judgment. By not judging the gift that a person gives, you help to maintain the purity of its form. By not judging yourself, you maintain your own purity and balance.

White Coral—Spiritual Aspects

Soul Tone: G, G# (both tones seem equally common)

Chakra Affinities: Throat (1)

Subtle Body Affinities: Emotional/Mental, Etheric, Spiritual

Energy Focus: Clearing

Element: Fire/Water

Cocreating with White Coral

When you are with family and friends, white coral can strengthen your self-esteem and help you clear judgment, frustration, and resentment relating to being told what to do. It can also aid you in letting go of the desire for recognition that can spur you on to give unwanted advice to others. White coral encourages you to affirm that you have something worthwhile to say, and to recognize yourself within.

White Coral Affirmation

"I LISTEN TO THAT WHICH IS FOR MY HIGHEST GOOD AND I RELEASE ALL ELSE."

The Red Coral Deva

Each lifestream needs to adopt an independent nature when other beings question or are directly critical of choices that are made. You need to be free of judgment so that you can function in a purity of flow. My energies help you to remain connected to your path in this life, regardless of the external experiences that may present themselves in opposition to your actions. I help you to move forward decisively, once you have assimilated what you need for taking your next step.

Red Coral—Spiritual Aspects

Soul Tone: E

Chakra Affinities: Solar Plexus (1)

Subtle Body Affinities: Emotional/Mental, Etheric, Spiritual

Energy Focus: Clearing

Element: Fire/Water

Cocreating with Red Coral

Red coral helps you resolve an experience where there has been conflict and criticism, and move forward decisively. It can clear the paralysis that can set in when you fear to make a move because of someone's disapproval. Sometimes the action you may need to take is to distance yourself from the source of confusion, and red coral can encourage you in this direction.

Red Coral Affirmation

"I HONOR BOTH MY OWN UNIQUE PATH AND THE UNIQUE PATHS OF OTHERS BY TAKING DECISIVE ACTION WITHOUT JUDGMENT."

Diamond

Physical Aspects

Diamond is pure carbon, with an isometric crystalline structure. Standing at 10 on the Mohs' scale, it is the hardest substance known. Only diamond will cut diamond. Diamond has a high ability to bend light (refraction) and to disperse light into its component colors. These properties are best brought out when the stone is cut and faceted. The brilliant cut, which has 32 facets plus the table (top flat surface) on the upper part, and 24 facets on the lower part, was especially developed to bring out the intense brilliance and fire of the diamond.

Diamonds form in igneous pipe-like cavities of a dark host rock called kimberlite. In South Africa diamonds are mined directly from the kimberlite. In Namibia and some other areas of Africa, diamonds are recovered from riverbeds of sand and rock where they have been released through erosion. More recently, diamonds have been extensively mined in Russia. Smaller deposits are in Brazil, India, and in the United States near Murfreesboro, Arkansas.

The Diamond Deva

I ask you to live according to the universal truths that are given in the ethical principals of all religions. I ask you to honor all life as it has been created, and as it is being expressed in all life forms. The Universal Truths are infinite. When you live with respect and kindness for all others, you will feel a continued connection with the Light of Truth. Knowing that you are always connected with the Light of Truth can give you the strength to act on the beliefs that you hold sacred, even when others oppose you. There are many who do not understand that the consequences of their selfish actions affect themselves and others even after they have left the Earth Plane. It is going to take your world a period of time before all will truly understand what I stand for.

Those of you on the Earth Plane who are learning about the accumulation of material possessions have much to learn from me. To possess me you pay a high monetary price. You have an opportunity to learn that trying to possess anything only blocks you from creatively receiving life-force energy. Those of you who lack the monetary resources to purchase me are learning something as well. You are learning that you can be in a state of non-attachment to things and still receive from me as you read these words. There is a need for an energy flow coming in and going out of your lives. You are given time and space to utilize your material energies, and then you must release your mental connection with those energies, whether or not their physical presence is released. In this way you will learn the constant presence of the Light of Truth in the ebb and flow of physical form.

Spiritual Aspects

Soul Tone: B

Chakra Affinities: Third Eye (1), Crown (2)

Subtle Body Affinities: Mental, Spiritual

Energy Focus: Building

Element: Air/Fire

Cocreating with Diamond

Diamond's physical hardness mirrors its spiritual quality of light-filled invincibility. Diamond purifies the will and encourages you to live according to a code of ethics that says to treat others as you would wish to be treated. You can use the diamond when you need the courage to act on your spiritual and moral convictions. With fiery directness, diamond encourages honesty with self and others. You have to let down your defenses in order to find diamond's truth and light.

Affirmation

"I TREAT OTHERS AS I WOULD LIKE TO BE TREATED."

Dioptase

Physical Aspects

The beautiful emerald green dioptase is a copper silicate that is often found with chrysocolla. It is softer than quartz, with a hardness of 5. Dioptase crystals are short prisms, capped by rhombihedrons that sparkle in the light, and it belongs to the hexagonal system. Dioptase is mined in Southwest African, Zaire, Colorado, and Arizona.

The Dioptase Deva

In this time of accelerated change, you are being asked to reclaim your personal self-expression, for you have brought a specific service to the earth plane. Your challenge is share your truth, and remain committed to it.

I teach you that self-judgment restricts you in the fulfillment of your life's purpose. Seek the Unconditional Love of Spirit to help you understand who you are, rather than seeking self-acceptance from others. Your entire being is filled with Light when you choose to be in the moment, in a state of non-judgment.

Without self-judgment you can recognize that you have unlimited possibilities of growth available to you, and you can choose with the guidance of Spirit, the beliefs and the actions that are right for you in the moment.

Spiritual Aspects

Soul Tone: F

Chakra Affinities: Heart, Throat, Solar Plexus, Root, Third Eye

Subtle Body Affinities: Mental/Spiritual

Energy Focus: Building

Element: Air/Earth

Cocreating with Dioptase

Dioptase seems like the wise grandfather who gives you practical advice on what you can do right now to release self-judgment. It can help you hear your Higher Self when self-dislike and self-criticism have short-circuited your connection. Dioptase can aid you in forgiving yourself and others, and in letting go of unrealistic expectations. Its earthy quality gives a supportive stability.

Affirmations

"I DISSOLVE THE VOICE OF MY INNER JUDGE WITH UNCONDITIONAL LOVE."

"I ACCEPT WHO I AM AND THE CHOICES I HAVE MADE."

Emerald

Physical Aspects

Emerald is a brilliant green member of the beryl family, which also includes aquamarine. It is a beryllium aluminum silicate that gets its green color from the trace mineral chromium. Emerald is slightly harder than quartz at 8 on the Mohs' scale, and it has a trigonal crystalline structure. Emerald crystals are six-sided and sometimes striated in appearance. Emerald develops in pegmatites and certain metamorphic rocks. Gem-quality deposits are located in several areas of Colombia, where the emerald veins are loosened with sticks and the emeralds picked out by hand. Other deposits are located in Brazil, South Africa, and the United States

The Emerald Deva

Through my energies you can experience the abundance of Unconditional Love and be healed by gratefully receiving that abundance. I can teach you about the larger meaning of prosperity. When you think that you are unworthy of any of the infinite forms of prosperity that are freely extended to you, you block the path of what you truly yearn for in this life. Anytime you increase your self-esteem or allow greater Light to enter your being, you are opening to prosperity. When you take care of your physical body, you are opening to prosperity. I know prosperity as energy that is always available, so one does not need to seek possession of it. When you try to "possess prosperity," it becomes elusive and passes between your fingers. You then become frustrated in your attempts to control or manipulate its energies. When you are feeling prosperous in a certain area of your life, are you at peace inside yourself at the same time? Or do you feel that you do not have enough? This thought form does not lead to fulfillment. Welcome the many forms of abundance in your life now and do not try to hold onto any one form of abundance. Understand that there is more than enough for all, and live with gratitude.

Spiritual Aspects

Soul Tone: F

Chakra Affinities: Heart (1), Third Eye, (2)

Subtle Body Affinities: Emotional/Mental, Spiritual, Etheric

Energy Focus: Building

Element: Air

Cocreating with Emerald

The energies of emerald are uplifting and healing, for they connect you with your Source. Emerald can increase your awareness of abundance in other forms than purely monetary, and encourages gratitude when you are dealing with issues of financial support. It can also contribute to your sense of feeling supported by Higher Guidance. There are times when acknowledging our abundance brings just the healing that we need.

Affirmation

"I JOYFULLY GIVE THANKS FOR THE ABUNDANCE IN MY LIFE."

Fire Agate

Physical Aspects

Agate is a banded microcrystalline quartz or silicon dioxide in the trigonal system. Fire agate, in particular, comes in various shades of opaque brown with orange-red tints. The most important deposits for agates in general are in southern Brazil and northern Uruguay. Agates are often found with the other quartz minerals such as amethyst and carnelian. Fire agate is fairly common and can be found in a number of other locations as well.

The Fire Agate Deva

>*Like fire, my energy can consume that which is no longer needed and move you forward with your focus on the larger picture. Lethargy is being in the state of idleness without a clear sense of connection to your energies and where they need to be focused in the next moment. Anything that remains in your energy system beyond its usefulness can create lethargy. My purpose is to clear that which you no longer need. My ultimate goal is to help you reconnect to your flow so that you have a sense of direction. Whether you experience my energies in a cathartic manner depends on you. When you are reconnected to your flow, there is greater space for new Unconditional Love to grow within you.*

Spiritual Aspects

Soul Tone: D

Chakra Affinities: Lower Abdomen (1), Root (2)

Subtle Body Affinities: Emotional/Mental, Etheric, Spiritual

Energy Focus: Clearing

Element: Fire/Earth

Cocreating with Fire Agate

Fire agate helps with *ambivalence,* whether it is lethargy relating to depression ("Monday morning blues") or wanting to remain in a space of the past. It strengthens physical vitality, cuts through sluggishness, and strengthens your will to focus on the present.

Affirmation

"I MOVE FORWARD WITH FOCUS AND DIRECTION AND AFFIRM THAT EVERY MOMENT IS A NEW BEGINNING."

Fluorite

Physical Aspects

Fluorite is calcium fluoride that comes in a variety of colors, including violet, pale blue, green, yellow, and clear. It has a hardness of 4 and belongs to the isometric crystalline system. Crystals of fluorite are cubic or octahedral in shape, and you can commonly find them for sale in these forms. Because fluorite has perfect cleavage in all four directions, it can also easily be cut into octahedrons. Sometimes fluorite is radiated to give it a more even *distribution* of color, and it can also be synthesized. Fluorite will glow violet when exposed to ultraviolet rays, which can be an identifying characteristic. Large deposits of fluorite are found in England, West Germany, Ontario, and the mid-western United States. We will discuss octahedral clear and purple fluorite.

The Clear Fluorite Deva

I help you to accept your physical vehicle and your life on this Earth Plane as a spiritual teacher for your growth. Whenever you feel limited by your physical state, I teach you to appreciate the present moment. When you wish you were somewhere else or you desperately want something you don't have, I encourage you to work with the essentials that are at hand. In this way I help you to quiet your will as well as your conscious mind. When your will is quiet, you are safe and protected, because there is nothing you need and you can be in a state of fulfillment. This state of fulfillment can provide an expanded awareness that prepares you for further learning.

Clear Fluorite—Spiritual Aspects

Soul Tone: A# for the clearest stones; A for stones with a bluish tinge.

Chakra Affinities: Third Eye (1), Root (1), Crown (1)

Subtle Body Affinities: Emotional/Mental, Spiritual, Etheric

Energy Focus: Clearing, Building depending on how you focus your intention.

Element: Air

Cocreating with Clear Fluorite

When you desire something strongly that may not be for your highest good, fluorite can help you release desire and focus your attention on the present moment. If you are getting caught in past memories and wishing for something that can no longer be, fluorite "disconnects the line" so that you are free to be in the here and now. Fluorite is helpful in meditation as you empty your mind and will, and it gives a sense of "the void." If you are feeling very disorganized, a few minutes with fluorite can bring a sense of order, balance, and stillness. You can hold fluorite before you work with the pendulum, tarot, or other tools with which you are seeking guidance. Fluorite can help you release your own opinions in the matter. Clear octahedral fluorite, combines well with other stones in layouts.

Clear Fluorite Affirmation

"I RELEASE MY PERSONAL WILL IN ORDER TO PURIFY MY AWARENESS."

The Purple Fluorite Deva

You can only become aware of higher aspects of your being when your etheric, emotional, and mental subtle bodies are in harmony with the specific purpose of expanding your spiritual understanding. Sometimes when you release your personal will, a void is created. In this void space you can see more clearly what you are not, which can then prepare you for integrating who you are. My purple vibration can give you a more specific understanding of the deeper mysteries of life. Through the use of my form we travel to higher levels of spiritual awareness in order to change how you perceive your physical reality. You can sense that there is more to your life than your observable circumstances. Through my energies I help you move from the world of form into the world of formlessness, where time as you know it is infinite and limitless. I move you beyond the purity of awareness to an expanded state of understanding the foundation of existence.

Purple Fluorite—Spiritual Aspects

Soul Tone: A, B (depending on your system of perception*)

Chakra Affinities: Third Eye (1)

Subtle Body Affinities: Emotional/Mental, Spiritual, Etheric

Energy Focus: Clearing, Building (depending on how you focus your intention)

Element: Air

Cocreating with Purple Fluorite

Purple fluorite is excellent for meditation because it prepares you by calming your desires and thoughts, and then takes you to higher levels of awareness. Its energies are very calming and peaceful, and it can move you beyond the space of pure awareness prepared by clear fluorite. It has less versatility in combination with other stones.

*Note: Purple fluorite is one mineral in which it seems that the soul tone can be perceived through more than one perspective. Our experience is that the combination of belief, your intuitive manner of perceiving, and the level on which you are functioning on your spiritual path all determine how you perceive the soul tone.

Purple Fluorite Affirmation

"As I merge with Divine Will I find greater peace and illumination."

Galena

Physical Aspects

Galena is a heavy, gray lead sulphide with a hardness of 2 1/2 and an isometric crystalline structure. Crystals are commonly found in the shapes of cubes and octahedrons. Galena is the most common of all lead minerals, and well-known deposits are found in Oklahoma, Kansas, and Missouri.

The Galena Deva

I work more broadly with your energy system to help you provide the specific focus or center that is most appropriate for you at that moment. When you have been in a meditative state, I can help you become more rooted in your physical body so that you can integrate what you have learned on your spiritual journey. If your thoughts tend to scatter in many directions, or if you are feeling loose ends emotionally, my focusing energy can help you establish your priorities.

To effectively ground the energies that are being transmitted from outside your energy fields requires that I be able to harmonize with the entire spectrum of frequencies. Whereas clear quartz crystal works to expand your existing energies, my purpose is to align your energy field into your physical vehicle. You see, energies are stepped down as they move from higher to lower levels. To function in this capacity I need to match my energies to the predominant tone for each energy center.

Spiritual Aspects
Soul Tone: All tones
Chakra Affinities: None
Subtle Body Affinities: Emotional/Mental, Etheric
Energy Focus: Building
Element: Earth

Cocreating with Galena

Galena does not have an affinity with a specific chakra. It can be held, utilized in meditation, or taken as an essence for any situation in which you need to settle, focus, or ground your energies. Galena can quiet your system before you go to bed, and is also useful if you feel spacey. It can also keep your thought-energies on a linear path when you are doing mental work. Galena can help a client calm extraneous thoughts before a session, and ground them after a session. You do not usually need an extended period of time with galena for centering to take place.

Affirmation

"I INTEGRATE MY SPIRITUAL AWARENESS BY ESTABLISHING MY PRIORITIES AND ACTING ON THEM."

Garnet

Physical Aspects

The name garnet applies to a group of aluminum silicate minerals that differ mainly in the substitution of one mineral element in their compositions. All garnets have a hardness of 7–7 1/2 and are isometric in their crystalline structure. Garnet crystals can occur in the form of dodecahedrons or trapezohedrons. The most well-known gem-quality garnet is pyrope garnet, which is an intense red, sometimes with shades or orange or brown. Gem-quality pyrope garnet comes from Arizona and Utah, as well as from Czechoslovakia and South Africa. Rhodolite is a variety of pyrope garnet that is rose red to pale violet and comes from North Carolina and Zaire.

Almandine garnet is deep red with violet tints. The stones are usually cut as cabochons with the back hollowed out so that they are thinner and therefore lighter in color. Garnets cut in this manner are called carbuncles. Almandine garnet is found in Alaska, Idaho, Brazil, and Australia. We have worked with the pyrope and rhodolite garnets.

The Garnet Deva

There are times when you of the Human Kingdom need a tangible experience to recognize the strength that is present within you. My energies provide a tangible experience that can extend into your physical body and give the sense of life-force energies built up inside you. When you seek support for your efforts, I tell you to look within. My purpose is to guide you to that place within that can provide reassurance whenever you need it. Once you have felt this reservoir of energy within you, the opportunity to return to its source will always be present.

Spiritual Aspects

Soul Tone: C

Chakra Affinities: Root (1)

Subtle Body Affinities: Emotional/Mental, Etheric, Spiritual

Energy Focus: Building

Element: Earth

Cocreating with Garnet

If you are in a time of change or anxiety and feeling a little lost, garnet can provide a sense of rootedness that helps you focus practically on one step at a time. Garnet gives a sense of expanding strength in your capacity to reach a goal. Your protection is the affirmation of your own solid core. If you are inclined to rush around in too many directions and at too fast a pace, garnet can slow you down and help you prioritize your activities. Garnet will help you feel less depleted of vitality at the completion of your tasks.

Affirmation

"I AFFIRM MY RESERVOIR OF INNER STRENGTH AND I ACT WITH PRACTICALITY."

Gem Silica

Physical Aspects

Gem silica is a gem quality chrysocolla or hydrous copper silicate. It is more translucent, like a tropical turquoise sea. Its more common cousin chrysocolla is more opaque.

The Gem Silica Deva

I help you connect with your spiritual purpose in being, the service you are giving, and what you are expressing to the world through your heart. I can assist you when your path of service seems difficult or unclear, and you experience sadness, disillusionment, or loss of hope and optimism. Sometimes it is your challenge to trust the unfoldment of your purpose, even when you can't see the Light at the end of the tunnel. I can give you a deep compassion and peace that comes when you trust that you are truly fulfilling your purpose in this life.

Spiritual Aspects

Soul Tone: A#

Chakra Affinities: Third Eye, Throat, Heart

Subtle Body Affinities: Spiritual

Energy Focus: Building

Element: Air, Water

Cocreating with Gem Silica

Gem silica opens you to the wider perspective of how your unique gifts help humankind to evolve in spiritual consciousness, so that you can better understand the meaning of your daily activities. It reminds you that each purpose is fulfilled in its own time. Compassion and acceptance are the result of releasing judgments about what you are doing in comparison with what others are doing, or what you thought you were about in this life. Peace and serenity are the gifts of gem silica, when you know that Spirit welcomes your service with joy. You do indeed make a difference and you are encouraged to give the best that you can give.

Affirmations

"I AFFIRM MY SPIRITUAL PURPOSE IN THE WORLD."

"I EXPRESS MY LIGHT WITH JOY AND TRUST."

Heliodor

Physical Aspects

Heliodor is a variety of beryl. By definition of the gem trade, green beryls are called emeralds and light blue beryls are called aquamarines. The name heliodor is given to the yellow and golden beryls. The beryl family is hexagonal (trigonal) with a hardness of 8, making them harder than quartz crystal. Heliodor was discovered in 1910 in Nambibia, but it has been found in the United States in New England, North Carolina, and California. It is often found with aquamarine in pegmatites and certain metamorphic rocks.

The Heliodor Deva

I interact with the human energy system to integrate your mental mind with the Higher Wisdom of Spirit. When you live predominantly through your mental mind, you are disconnected from the wisdom that helps you move through change without pain. I assist you into a space of greater receptivity to new beliefs. I also help you release the self-judgment that may hold you back from trying something new. You strengthen your will to change by bringing greater clarity and spiritual perspective to your understanding.

Growth involves learning to reach beyond initial definitions of who you believe you are and what you believe that you can do. I can provide the trust that allows you to move through the void of the unknown into the Greater Light that can illuminate your experience. When you understand how taking a particular step contributes to your growth and your connection with Spirit, it becomes easier to think and act in new ways, without self-judgment.

Spiritual Aspects

Soul Tone: A#

Chakra Affinities: Third Eye

Subtle Body Affinities: Mental/Spiritual

Energy Focus: Clearing

Element: Air

Cocreating with Heliodor

Heliodor's sedative effect can assist you in making mental changes where you are open to the alternative course of action, but you are reluctant to give up what you currently believe. You can work with it by asking for clarification on a particular course of action. For example, I asked for guidance from the heliodor about the idea of staying home, rather than taking a trip that I was looking forward, but also involved extra time and money. What I learned was that by truly appreciating the fulfillment of my present space, I could dissipate the emotion-backed belief that I need experience and adventure in order to grow and be at peace. I could learn to Be through being, not doing. Heliodor's golden light is like an inner beacon that gently and calmly calls you into yourself, to find the stillness of Higher Wisdom.

Affirmation

> "I REACH FOR THE LIGHT OF GREATER WISDOM TO ASSIST ME IN CHANGING MY BELIEFS."

Hematite

Physical Aspects

Hematite is the principal ore of iron, and is most often sold as a polished, shiny, steel gray stone. Rough hematite is distinguished by the blood red to reddish-brown streak that it leaves when scratched on a hard surface. It is an opaque, iron oxide of the hexagonal (trigonal) system, with a hardness of 5–6. The name hematite derives from the Greek word meaning blood, because of the red color of the powdered stone. Cutting material comes from England, Russia, Switzerland, Italy, and Brazil, as well as several locations in the United States.

The Hematite Deva

I help to soften the severity of emotional pain so that your experiences do not feel as devastating. With less emotional pain you will find it easier to take responsibility toward redirecting your actions. My energies also help to break the pattern of thought that says, "The present will be like the past. Things always happen this way for me." When the perceived continuity between experiences is broken, you can begin to change your thoughts about failing or feeling like a failure. When you choose to release emotional pain, I can help you redirect your energy into a more balanced state. Rather than being an observer where experiences happen to you, I encourage you to utilize your emotional energy in more effective ways. I help you to value yourself, and to become your own counsel for strength.

Spiritual Aspects
Soul Tone: F
Chakra Affinities: Root, Lower Abdomen, Solar Plexus
Subtle Body affinities: Emotional/Mental
Energy Focus: Clearing/Building
Element: Earth/Water

Cocreating with Hematite
Hematite can feel like a sedative that provides more emotional stability. It helps to remove the intensity of emotional pain that seems out of control. It can balance the extremes of mood swings, when you are emotionally drained. Its steadiness removes you from the immediacy of an experience so that you can find a broader perspective and rebuild your self-esteem.

Affirmation

"As I release emotional pain, I am freed to take action."

Iolite

Physical Aspects
Iolite is the gem trade name for translucent, blue and violet cordierite. Cordierite can also be brown or black, and is usually found in a massive or granular form, as crystals are very rare. Iolite is a magnesium aluminum silicate with a hardness of 7–7 1/2 and an orthorhombic crystalline structure. Its colors can change from various shades of blue to gray as it is viewed from different directions. Iolite is generally associated with metamorphic rocks and mined in Burma and Brazil. Cordierite can be found in Connecticut and in various areas of the Northwest.

The Iolite Deva

I link you directly into your Soul so that you can understand why you are here, and receive healing energy from lessons that you have already learned. The Soul is the composite energy memory of your being, which has no past, present, or future, though past, present and future are contained within it. From your Higher Self you can receive specific guidance that is more ideally suited to the practical Earth Plane world. What is received from the Soul is the state of being where you live in Oneness. The Soul retains only the purest vibrations as you pass from one lifetime to another. The subconscious mind contains a record of areas where your Soul seeks to refine itself. Your Soul is therefore an integration of your purest qualities, perfectly balanced and ordered. It is through persistent intention that you can deepen your connection with your Soul.

There are several ways you can work with me to access the energy of your Soul for healing. One is to first decide on a spiritual quality that you are trying to understand and master in your personal growth. Every spiritual quality has a specific frequency, and that frequency is then transmitted to you by your Soul. Another way is to ask your Soul to be present with you as you release what is no longer needed on your path. Your Soul then becomes a companion in your process, and you can be receptive to the qualities transmitted to you. I then guide you to integrate what you have received into your daily life.

Spiritual Aspects

Soul Tone: B

Chakra Affinities: Third Eye (1), Crown (1)

Subtle Body Affinities: Spiritual

Energy Focus: Spiritual Expansion

Element: Air

Cocreating with Iolite

Connecting with your Soul through iolite is like *being* in a total state of Unconditional Love rather than merely thinking or feeling Unconditional Love. Iolite also gives a total sense of protection as you receive the energy you need. Take the essence as a preparation for a meditation in which you connect with your Soul.

Affirmation

"I OPEN TO GREATER PERSONAL AND SPIRITUAL GROWTH THROUGH COMMUNICATION WITH MY SOUL."

Jade

Physical Aspects

The name jade is applied to two different opaque minerals, jadeite and nephrite. They have similar characteristics and are very difficult to distinguish. Both types have a hardness of 6 1/2–7 and they are very tough, which makes them ideal for carving. Jadeite and nephrite have a monoclinic crystalline structure. They come in many shades of green as well as black, red, brown, white, and green spotted with white.

Jadeite is rarer and is a sodium aluminum silicate. The most well-known deposits are in Burma, Guatemala, Japan, Mexico, and the United States. Nephrite is found in China, Australia, Brazil, Canada, and Mexico. There are jade triplets on the market, and sometimes jade is dyed to make it a more emerald-like transparent green.

We refer to the nephrite jade below.

The Nephrite Jade Deva

I promote the practice of detachment from the emotional body of the lifestream. I further encourage selective, focused thought. When you are seeking clarity in the mind I can help you release extraneous thoughts and emotions, so that you can maintain the discipline of being centered and balanced. My energies truly complement any spiritual practice.

Spiritual Aspects

Soul Tone: E
Chakra Affinities: Solar Plexus (1), Heart (1), Third Eye (1)
Subtle Body Affinities: Emotional/Mental, Spiritual, Etheric
Energy Focus: Building, Clearing
Element: Earth/Air

Cocreating with Nephrite Jade

Jade's focused, calm balance is versatile in its effects. In past-life and dream work, jade moves slowly but deeply, and can help you detach from the emotions involved so that you can see more clearly. If you are emotionally oversensitive, jade can provide balance if used on an ongoing basis. It is also useful in mental work in which clear judgment and focus are important. Jade can also prepare you for meditation by calming and stilling your mind. It is an aid in promoting a more effortless discipline of any skill.

Affirmation

"MY BODY, MIND, AND SPIRIT ARE IN PERFECT BALANCE."

Jasper

Physical Aspects

Some geologists include jasper in the microcrystalline quartz family called chalcedony. Within the jasper group are such trade names as picture jasper, agate jasper, and Egyptian jasper. Petrified wood has a mineral composition of jasper, chalcedony, and frequently, opal. Our intuitive observations are based on the opaque, red jasper, although yellow, green and brown jasper are fairly common.

As a member of the quartz family, jasper belongs to the hexagonal system and has a hardness of 6 1/2–7. The name jasper is derived from a Greek word meaning "spotted stone," which aptly describes its spotted, striped, or mottled appearance. Jasper is mined in the United States as well as in Europe, Russia, and Brazil.

The Jasper Deva

I challenge you to increase your self-confidence through creative expression. This process teaches you to release self-judgment and value your unique abilities. My energies are especially helpful in stimulating a deeper sensitivity to your inner and outer resources. Remember that you are expressing an aspect of yourself, rather than trying to create something for another's recognition. As you create, you will recognize more deeply the fullness of your capacities, and increase your compassion for self and others. You will also trust more completely in the unfoldment of your growth.

Spiritual Aspects

Soul Tone: C#

Chakra Affinities: Root, Lower Abdomen

Subtle Body Affinities: Emotional/Mental

Energy Focus: Building

Element: Fire

Cocreating with Jasper

Jasper's fire quickens your awareness of your physical senses and the joy of being alive, so that you can move from a surface connection with your activities to a deeper involvement. It stimulates enthusiasm, physical energy, and zest that can counter listlessness, despondency, or disinterest in daily affairs. If you are recuperating from physical illness, or feeling that nothing really matters, jasper can help you find meaning in your present circumstances by heightening your physical awareness and vitality. Your attention may be called to beauty that you hadn't noticed before, and your sense of joy in being alive is deepened. Jasper stimulates creative expression as a means of participating more fully in life.

Affirmation

"I CREATIVELY EXPRESS THE JOY OF BEING ALIVE, IN EVERYTHING THAT I DO."

Jet

Physical Aspects

Jet is a bituminous coal of hardness 3–4. When polished it takes on a velvety, waxy luster, and when rubbed it becomes electrically charged. Jet is inexpensive, but watch out for imitations. Black tourmaline, chalcedony, obsidian, glass, garnet, rubber, onyx, and other types of coal have all been marketed as jet. The most well-known source of jet comes from Whitby, in

Yorkshire England. Jet is also mined in Spain, France, and in the United States in Utah and Colorado.

The Jet Deva

My purpose is to help you process grief by moving you to a state of resolution about a death experience. I can be a catalyst for connecting with your loved one so that the illusion of the separation of physical form becomes transformed into the peace of unity. Through me you know that the bridge between yourself and the one who has moved into Spirit is forever whole and complete. By integrating this knowledge you become free to move forward on your own spiritual journey, sustained by the compassionate love of Spirit.

Spiritual Aspects

Soul Tone: C#

Subtle Body Affinities: Emotional/Spiritual

Energy Focus: Building

Element: Water/Air

Cocreating with Jet

Jet gives a quality of grounding and nurturing that also encourages the acceptance of the inevitability of change. When you are denying that a relationship or experience has ended, jet can assist you in acknowledging that a purpose has been fulfilled and that it is time to let go. Rather than pushing away death, allow yourself to explore your feelings. Releasing a loved one can threaten you with emptiness and lack. Jet counsels you to remember that only a form is shifting, not your essential core of Oneness with Spirit. Jet weaves the paradoxical energies of constant change and the eternal peace of Spirit, into a tapestry of acceptance that you can experience as resolution and balance.

Affirmation

"I ACCEPT BOTH THE REALITY OF CHANGE, AND MY ETERNAL ONENESS WITH SPIRIT."

Kunzite

Physical Aspects

Kunzite is a pink-violet, gem-quality member of the spodumene family. It is a lithium aluminum silicate with a hardness of 6–7 and a monoclinic crystalline structure. Kunzite cleaves well in two directions, making it very sensitive to pressure and therefore difficult to cut. It has strong pleochroism, which means that it shows lighter and darker shades of pink-violet when viewed from different directions. Spodumene is found in pegmatite veins along with beryl and tourmaline, and it occasionally forms large crystals. Gem quality kunzite comes from California and Maine, and also from Brazil and Madagascar. We have also utilized clear kunzite, which might be more accurately called "clear spodumene."

The Lavender-pink Kunzite Deva

In all things and in all ways, live your life to its fullest, both in the affairs of the physical plane and in the exploration of the higher spiritual realms. Know that you are truly an unlimited being and there is no end to what you can create. The self-denial that has been practiced in the religions of your world has served its purpose in its time. However, self-denial has undertones of constriction that go beyond the process of purification. Whether you deny yourself certain things or hoard your physical possessions, the result is that energies are locked in place and are not free to move. I say that what is needed now is an expansion of life-force energies rather than a containment of their form. When you work with me you may feel "speeded up," because I dissolve any fears or hesitancy and I accelerate your willingness to enjoy and create new opportunities. When you expand your life-force energies by creating your life to the fullest, you benefit all life on this planet.

Those of you who are attracted to me are opening your intuitive sensitivity and making a commitment to continue that unfoldment. When you listen to me through your inner sensitivity, I commit you to moderation as well as expansion so that your life-force energies are in balance as you accelerate your capaci-

ties. You will find that your energies are channeled into more activities that are filled with Light and Unconditional Love.

Lavender-pink Kunzite—Spiritual Aspects

Soul Tone: F

Chakra Affinities: Heart (1)

Subtle Body Affinities: Emotional/Mental, Spiritual, Etheric

Energy Focus: Building

Element: Water/Fire

Cocreating with Lavender-pink Kunzite

Kunzite can speed up a desire to create more beauty and fulfillment in your life. It heightens a desire to participate in activities in which you grow and receive in new ways. Kunzite also accelerates your creative potential and the desire to express that potential. You can work with it when you feel stuck or constricted in your self-expression. It will help you to understand the difference between moderation and constriction and will increase your enthusiasm and zest for life.

Lavender-pink Kunzite Affirmation

"I LIVE MY LIFE ZESTFULLY AND CREATIVELY TO THE FULLEST."

Clear Kunzite Deva

Those of you who are drawn to my energies will choose the lavender-pink variety or the clear variety according to whether you will blend my energies at your heart and third eye, or work with me primarily at your third eye. I can teach you to expand the ways in which you work with your third eye energies. I can help you move beyond projecting energies and into higher frequencies where you work with life-force energies before they are created into solid physical substance. You are then learning about creativity at a higher level. You are truly unlimited in your ability to create.

Clear Kunzite—Spiritual Aspects

Soul Tone: A

Chakra Affinities: Third Eye (1)

Subtle Body Affinities: Emotional/Mental, Spiritual, Etheric

Energy Focus: Building

Element: Water/Fire

Cocreating with Clear Kunzite

The energies are similar in purpose to lavender-pink kunzite, except that they feel more active and perhaps focus more on understanding creativity in the spiritual realms. Our experience with both the lavender-pink and the clear kunzite is that it can stimulate the desire nature and also the desire to want everything *now*. When working with kunzite, ask about timing for pursuing your activities. Ask, "Is this the time for me to pursue for my optimal balance?"

Clear Kunzite Affirmation

"I CREATE TO MY HIGHEST CAPACITY MY VISION OF LIGHT."

Kyanite

Physical Aspects

Kyanite is a translucent blue aluminum silicate. Along its axis the hardness is 4 1/2, and perpendicular to its axis it is 6–7. Kyanite is a member of the triclinic crystalline family. Because of its variable hardness and its sensitivity to pressure, kyanite is difficult to cut. The crystals are shaped like long, flat blades with irregular streaks of differing shades of blue and brown. Kyanite is a metamorphic rock often found in gneiss and schist. The most striking blues come from Switzerland. Other deposits are located in North Carolina, Burma, Brazil, and Austria.

The Kyanite Deva

I seek for you to become aware of how to work with finer levels of life-force energy for physical healing. When you hold my energies or internalize them, I take you to a level where you

have a panoramic view of what your physical vehicle is really like, and where you can visually perceive its structure and sense its life-force energies. When your spiritual subtle body is activated, you can learn how to direct your energies so that they positively impact on the physical vehicle. With this knowledge you are encouraged to take appropriate action to restore the balance within. As you learn to better understand how the physical vehicle is an expression for spiritual perfection, your lifestyle will reflect a new balance. You will also work with the physical healing process in a more sensitive and finely tuned manner.

Spiritual Aspects

Soul Tone: A#

Chakra Affinities: Crown (1), Third Eye (1)

Subtle Body Affinities: Spiritual, Etheric

Energy Focus: Spiritual Expansion

Element: Air

Cocreating with Kyanite

Kyanite can aid you when you are dialoguing with your physical body in meditation. It affirms a sense of the Divinity and sacredness of the physical body, so that it can be easier to make healthy lifestyle changes. Kyanite's life-force energy can open the way for spiritual healing of the body if you work consciously with the idea that your body is a sacred temple and a manifestation of Love.

Affirmation

"MY PHYSICAL BODY IS A SACRED TEMPLE, BUILT OF PURE LOVE."

Labradorite

Physical Aspects

Labradorite is an opaque gray stone that shimmers with a metallic play of colors, especially greens and blues, when you hold it at certain angles. It was first discovered in the Canadian province of Labrador in

1770. Labradorite is a sodium, calcium, aluminum, silicate member of the feldspar family. Similar to other feldspars, it has a hardness of 6–6 1/2 and a triclinic crystalline structure. The labradorite discovered in Finland in the early 1940s has a particularly wide variety of color and is sometimes sold under the trade name of "spectrolite." As well as Canada and Finland, labradorite is mined in the Malagasy Republic, Mexico, Russia, and the United States

The Labradorite Deva

When you are reaching a crossroads in life, I can bring greater light to your decision-making by helping you access the Akashic Records. The Akashic Records are the ultimate collection of all experiences from the very minute to the infinite. Experiences are stored as thought and feeling energy in the etheric forms of clear quartz crystal. Clear quartz crystal, as you know, has an infinite capacity to store energy. When you access the Akashic Records, you are an observer, receiving a pure picture of an experience, with its spiritual message as well as its physical, mental, or emotional content. In order to access the Akashic Records, your intent must be to apply the knowledge to your personal and spiritual growth. Otherwise the knowledge will not be made available to you.

Both your subconscious mind and the Akashic Records are repositories of what has transpired through time. One difference is that your subconscious will carry information from more recent lifetime experiences. It is closer at hand and therefore more pertinent. You can also participate more fully in the details, beliefs, and feelings of the experience. With the Akashic Records you can go back to the very beginning of the existence. The scope of information is much broader. Accessing the Records can be helpful when you have accessed the subconscious mind and there is a sense that something more is needed.

When working with the Akashic Records, you might ask to be shown when you exhibited specific spiritual qualities and manifested them in their highest order and form. You can then ask that they be connected into your energy system so that they

can be applied in your present life. If you have had difficulties with a particular person, you might ask to see what has transpired, and how the optimal healing can be achieved. This can be like a past-life experience, but you observe it more impersonally and you receive a broader panoramic overview of the spiritual lessons involved. You can also ask to be shown what a particular situation could look like when the blocks are totally removed from the experience. The changes indicated could involve action or a change in belief or perception about the experience.

You can refer to me as the timeless teacher, for I can take you on a journey into what was, what is, and what can be.

Spiritual Aspects
Soul Tone: B

Chakra Affinities: Third Eye (1), Crown (1)

Subtle Body Affinities: Spiritual

Energy Focus: Spiritual expansion

Element: Air

Cocreating with Labradorite

Utilize the essence or the stone for a meditation to access the Akashic Records. With labradorite you can inquire about the past to support your present. You can also ask to receive information that is related to your spiritual purpose.

Affirmation

"I NOW ACCESS THE AKASHIC RECORDS IN ORDER TO EXPAND MY SPIRITUAL GROWTH."

Lapis Lazuli

Physical Aspects

Lapis lazuli, or lapis for short, is actually an opaque conglomerate of dark blue lazurite streaked with white calcite, or sprinkled with gold specks of pyrite. Lapis may also include small quantities of augite, diopside, mica, and hornblende. This mixture is found when sodium, aluminum, and calcium combine but lack sufficient silica to form a feldspar. Lapis belongs to the isometric crystalline system and has a hardness of 5–6.

The finest lapis, with an intense, uniform blue, comes from Afghanistan. One of the ways that it is mined is to light a fire on the host limestone rock, which is then put out with water. The sudden change in temperature weakens the limestone rocks, which can then be broken away with hammers. The pockets of lapis can then be lifted out with crowbars. Lapis is also found in Siberia and Chile. The color of Chilean lapis is less intense and has larger streaks of white calcite. Lapis has been found in this country in Colorado and California. Swiss lapis is an imitation stone made from staining jasper with a Prussian blue dye.

The Lapis Lazuli Deva

> *I penetrate thought energy that may seem "rational" but is in truth non-essential, so that you can see clearly what may actively be affecting your energy system. I encourage your presence with me in this process so that you can become more focused in your mind. Whenever you seek to clear anything that is stored within your subconscious mind, I ask you to formulate a question that relates to what is occurring in the present moment. I utilize this energy pattern to pinpoint the area of the subconscious where its energy counterpart is stored. Throughout this process, I emphasize "clear sight." I help you then to move into a space where you initiate action to make the changes that need to be made.*

Spiritual Aspects

Soul Tone: G#, A (stones with more white calcite may test G# and deeper blue lapis tests A)

Chakra Affinities: Third Eye (1)

Subtle Body Affinities: Mental, Spiritual

Energy Focus: Clearing, Building

Element: Fire/Earth

Cocreating with Lapis Lazuli

With its steady, penetrating energy, lapis helps you look at things you have been avoiding. Spiritually, it strengthens the desire for truth. When you are ill and don't know why, lapis is one of the stones that can help you become aware of the issues. Lapis essence can be taken before past-life work or for spiritual purification. Lapis with more white calcite is calmer and steadier in its energies, while lapis with more pyrite gives fiery overtones.

Affirmation

"I SEEK THE TRUTH IN UNDERSTANDING MY EXPERIENCES."

Larimar

Physical Aspects

Larimar is the trade name for gem-quality blue pectolite. Pectolite comes in other colors, including clear, white, green, and pink. It is a sodium calcium silicate with a hardness of 4 1/2–5 and a triclinic crystalline structure. The beautiful blue of larimar comes from traces of copper. Pectolite is not generally considered to be gem material because it is normally found as a loose aggregate not cohesive enough to cut. However, larimar has more compact fibers and can take a high polish, which sometimes gives a cat's-eye effect (an effect resembling the slit eye of a cat caused by the reflection of light by parallel fibers). Larimar is considered rare, because it is found only in the Dominican Republic. Other colors of pectolite are found in Scotland, Sweden, Canada, Alaska, and Arkansas.

We have worked with a larimar that is a robin's-egg blue.

The Larimar Deva

Deep inside many of you there is a yearning to express your greater spiritual service in a more original, diverse manner. My energies act as a catalyst to bring this energy and awareness into your consciousness, where you can then move with it. I encourage a pioneering spirit, welcome unusual insights, and seek to express them without desire for recognition. Do not be concerned if what you say is not understood by those around you, for you truly may be working from a different level. Perhaps you are ahead of your time. What I bring is strength and reassurance that you are truly on your path, when you sense yourself as separated from the masses. Do not seek recognition from others. Your recognition comes from the greater service that you give. It is an inner sense of fulfilling your spiritual purpose. You are learning how unlimited you truly are.

You ask me why I am relatively rare. I say to you that as more and more lifestreams seek to express from their higher spiritual service, those that are in need of my energies will indeed find me.

Spiritual Aspects

Soul Tone: G

Chakra Affinities: Throat (1)

Subtle Body Affinities: Emotional/Mental, Spiritual, Etheric

Energy Focus: Building

Element: Fire

Cocreating with Larimar

Larimar can be useful as a confidence builder when you are involved in an ongoing spiritual service project that involves doing something in a new way. Examples would be starting a unique service that helps people in some manner, or experimenting with a way to conserve a natural resource. Larimar helps you to move out of conventional ways of thinking and doing things so that you are free to dream up innovative possibilities. Larimar can be excellent for brainstorming, when you need to come up with ways to manifest a particular service that has been in the back of your mind for a long time. Larimar's energies strengthen your desire to express a unique service, rather than simply expanding your mental creativity.

Affirmation

"I FULFILL MY SPIRITUAL SERVICE IN A WAY THAT IS UNIQUELY MY OWN, IN ORDER TO HELP OTHERS UNDERSTAND THE UNLIMITED NATURE OF GROWTH AND KNOWLEDGE."

Lepidolite

Physical Aspects

Lepidolite is a translucent stone that is sold most often in pinky-lilac shades. The name comes from the Greek word *lepidos* meaning *scale*, which refers to its occurrence as tiny granules of crystals on top of a quartz conglomerate. It also appears in thin layers, like lilac-colored mica.

Lepidolite belongs to the monoclinic system and has a hardness of 2–3. It is mined as a source of lithium in New England, South Dakota, and southern California.

The Lepidolite Deva

I first soothe and quiet your emotional body so that you can then seek the principal understanding that underlies an experience. When you ride life like a roller coaster, you cannot create with a centered mind and a feeling heart. I help you create a balance in your life between a lighthearted spirit and a committed intent.

I can also assist you in discerning when it is time to go with the flow of events with true serenity, and when it is time to choose a different course of action. I can help you see more clearly how you need to release thoughts and patterns that you are not relevant to your current state of being. You need only to ask.

Spiritual Aspects

Soul Tone: granular—D#, mica-like—E

Chakra Affinities: Lower Abdomen, Solar Plexus, Heart

Subtle Body Affinities: Emotional/Mental

Energy Focus: Clearing/Building

Element: Water/Air

Cocreating with Lepidolite

Lepidolite is a very useful diagnostic stone. When holding it or placing it on your body, you can ask what emotion-backed thoughts are impeding your growth at this time. It can show you a picture of how you are reacting to your life at the moment, in a way that also points in the direction of balance.

Lepidolite also has a sedative effect, so that when you are feeling overstimulated, it supports you in regaining a sense of calm and balance. It asks you to slow down a little, relax, and take events in your stride. Lepidolite reminds you that time passes, and a smile goes a long way.

Affirmation

> "I SHIFT MY FOCUS FROM STIMULATION TO BALANCE, IN ORDER TO ENJOY MY LIFE MORE FULLY."

Magnetite

Physical Aspects

Magnetite is a metallic, black iron oxide with a hardness of 5 1/2–6 1/2 and an isometric crystalline structure. It is one of the most abundant of all the oxide minerals and occurs in a variety of environments. A distinguishing physical characteristic is its magnetic property.

The Magnetite Deva

You have come to Planet Earth for infinite reasons. Your main purpose for being here is to grow and expand your spiritual awareness. I urge you to commit your total being to this process. Whenever you are having second thoughts about moving forward on your spiritual path, my energies can give you the needed push to go forward once again. Sometimes you may not truly comprehend why I am stimulating inner movement toward a particular outer manifestation. As your path continues to unfold, you will see why you were guided to move in a particular direction.

Spiritual Aspects
Soul Tone: C#
Chakra Affinities: Root (1)
Subtle Body Affinities: Emotional/Mental, Etheric
Energy Focus: Clearing, Building
Element: Water

Cocreating with Magnetite

Magnetite gently but directly propels you toward change. It gives a sense that change is inevitable and that it is something to which you can look forward. If you are reluctant or fearful about leaving a situation behind that seems familiar and secure, magnetite helps you to grow in a new way. If you have felt a sense of agitation or depression from people or a place, magnetite can give protection and aid you in releasing those feelings.

Affirmation

"I TRUST MY ABILITIES TO ACCELERATE CHANGE."

Malachite

Physical Aspects

Malachite is a layered green, opaque stone of the mono-clinic system. It is a basic copper carbonate containing eight percent water with a hardness of 3 1/2–4. Because it is a secondary copper mineral, it is often found with other copper carbonates such as azurite. The finest malachite comes from the Urals in Russia, Chile, Zaire, South Africa, and in this country, from Arizona. Malachite polishes to a silky luster, which has made it a popular choice for jewelry. It is sensitive to heat, acids, ammonia, and hot water. Malachite will lose its sheen if you soak it in salt water. You can clean it with salt or with some other method.

The Malachite Deva

Fear that appears as part of your experiences is not to be considered a sign of weakness, as you may have been taught. I see an initial step in uprooting fear from your being. That step is to understand why the fear has surfaced in the first place. When you understand the nature of this fear, it is unlikely to resurface, once its imbalance has been removed from the energy field. Fear can be very tenacious and stubborn, so more intensified energies are well suited for accomplishing this order of service to the Human Kingdom. When you feel immobilized by fear, I give you courage and strengthen your resolve to be more than you thought you could be.

Spiritual Aspects

Soul Tone: E or F depending on the individual stone.

Chakra Affinities: Solar Plexus (1), Heart (1), Lower Abdomen (2)

Subtle Body Affinities: Emotional/Mental, Etheric, Spiritual

Energy Focus: Clearing

Element: Fire/Earth

Cocreating with Malachite

Malachite, with its intense probing action, can help you break free from limitations related to fear, guilt, or self-denial. It increases both determination and courage in any situation because it helps dissolve acute fear and anxiety. Malachite is an invaluable aid when you are working on the release of old, limiting habit patterns.

Affirmation

"I HAVE THE COURAGE AND DETERMINATION TO WORK THROUGH ALL FEAR."

Moldavite

Physical Aspects

Moldavite is a trade name for green tektite. Tektites are meteorite "glass" fragments that range from a million to a billion years old. They vary in size from microscopic to the size of an orange. Chemically, tektites are silicon dioxide plus aluminum oxide. They register 5 1/2 on the hardness scale and have an amorphous crystalline structure. This amorphous structure, with its large bubbles and swirls, suggests that their shape and size is due to rapid heating followed by cooling upon entry into our atmosphere. Tektites are normally brown and black in color; the translucent green moldavites are found only in Czechoslovakia. Moldavite is rare and therefore more expensive than many stones.

The Moldavite Deva

My purpose is twofold. The first purpose is to expand your understanding of who you are in relationship to the universe. The second is to be a vehicle for you to enter into other dimensions of reality for a greater understanding of life. The quality of my energy has a releasing effect, so that when you understand your true nature, you can move out of limited thinking to a greater knowledge of Self. Let me give you an example to explain what I am saying. You are told that you must limit certain physical activities, and you have accepted that viewpoint as being totally true for you. My energies enlarge your perception of who you are, so that you can choose to renew your efforts to pursue these activities, or you can choose to no longer feel limited by your circumstances.

In addition to bringing awareness of the Greater Light within yourself so that you can expand beyond limited personal thinking, I can help you connect to the infinite wisdom that lies outside your being. All forms of life are interconnected, and you have the capacity to communicate with the intelligence on other planets and stars, where time no longer exists as you know it.

The process of interdimensional communication works in the following manner. Signals are sent as energy from your Higher Self mind into interdimensional space and are received by Light Beings who have refined the spiritual tool of telepathic thought transference. The nature of your contact is perceived and moves through channels until the right spiritual entity is found to answer your inquiry. Once the channels are connected between the spiritual entity and your Higher Self mind, then the process of communication can begin. Sometimes your Higher Self may be able to channel this knowledge directly into your conscious mind. Whether this is done instantaneously or in a selected space of time is in direct relationship to the openness and receptivity of your conscious mind. Just as patience is a significant lesson that you are learning while living on the Earth Plane, patience is required by anyone seeking to establish contact with Light Beings in other dimensions. A prerequisite is to let go of any comparisons between yourself and any other Light Being. Remember that the process of learning and growth is taking place in other realities as well. Remember to communicate a pure sense of thankfulness to the Light Being with whom you share time and space in this process. Unconditional Love knows no bonds and is thus a cosmic, universal concept in all dimensions. Utilize the quality of Light in all forms of communication with Light Beings.

Two things are achieved by seeking to expand to other dimensional levels. First, there is an understanding that there are other lifestreams with the capacity to assist you and your Planet in its evolutionary cycle. Second, there is an activation that takes place within your own mind that helps you to create more solutions to the imbalance currently on your Planet. I work co-creatively in this capacity with clear quartz crystal. The goal, you see, is to expand your access to greater knowing.

Spiritual Aspects

Soul Tone: B (but will respond to F if the stone is put on the thymus gland)

Chakra Affinities: Thymus Gland (1), Third Eye (1), Crown (1)

Subtle Body Affinities: Spiritual, Etheric, Emotional/Mental

Energy Focus: Spiritual Expansion, Clearing Element: Air

Cocreating With Moldavite

If you feel "out of touch" with your spiritual connection, or you feel that your life is currently without spiritual meaning, moldavite can reconnect you spiritually. This reconnection will most likely involve change and regeneration, giving you an opportunity to drop limiting beliefs that are keeping you from receiving greater spiritual awareness.

You can also work with moldavite at your third eye and crown in meditation for interdimensional communications (see Chapter 7).

Moldavite Affirmation

"I GO BEYOND LIMITED THINKING AND RECEIVE THE UNCONDITIONAL LOVE PRESENT IN OTHER DIMENSIONS OF THE UNIVERSE."

Moonstone

Physical Aspects

Moonstone is a potassium aluminum silicate member of the feldspar family. It is a translucent, milky-white stone with a hardness of 6–6 1/2 and a monoclinic crystalline structure. The alternating layers of orthoclase and albite feldspars cause its shimmering effect. When these layers are thin and you hold a moonstone up to reflected light, you will see a beautiful blue-white glimmer. Moonstone is mined in Sri Lanka, Australia, Brazil, and the United States

The Moonstone Deva

I see the emotional body as holding the key to maintaining balance and wellness throughout your being. Each feeling you have passes through several stages before it has an impact on your physical vehicle. First the feeling becomes a presence that you may or may not be totally aware of. Second, as you become aware of your feelings, you examine them without acting on them. Third, you decide how you are going to respond to their presence.

The quality of your action depends on the acceptance of your feelings. If you feed life-force energy to a feeling of anger or sadness, your actions will carry the imbalanced energy. When this happens, the process of integrating the results of your actions takes more persistence and patience. I tell you through my energies that I love you unconditionally and that I understand the sensitive feeling space that you are in at the moment. I encourage an acceptance of what you are feeling so that you can then gently release the need for that experience. Accept yourself as you are, and know that you can creatively change yourself, not because of some external experience, but because it feels more right and peaceful inside of you to do so.

Spiritual Aspects

Soul Tone: G#, A (depending on the individual stone)

Chakra Affinities: Third Eye (1), Solar Plexus (1)

Subtle Body Affinities: Emotional/Mental, Etheric, Spiritual

Energy Focus: Clearing, Building

Element: Water

Cocreating with Moonstone

Moonstone can help you accept what you are feeling when you need to release emotional tension. It has a calm, flowing peace that helps restore emotional balance in everyday experiences, such as worry or over-reaction to a situation. Moonstone can help you better understand dreams that are telling you about your emotional state of balance. With moonstone you may also respond more sensitively to the emotional nature of others.

Affirmation

"I VALUE MY EMOTIONAL SENSITIVITY, KNOWING THAT IT IS ALL RIGHT TO FEEL WHAT I AM FEELING."

Moss Agate

Physical Aspects

Moss agate is a clear microcrystalline quartz with moss-green inclusions of hornblende. Scientifically it is not considered an agate because it is not layered. Like other quartz, it is silicon dioxide with a hardness of 7 and a trigonal crystalline structure. The best gem qualities come from India, but it is also found in China and the United States.

The Moss Agate Deva

My energies help you to attune to the Spiritual Consciousness in all forms of life found within the Kingdoms of Nature. I help you understand that opening to the world of Spirit means receiving the Unconditional Love that is Consciousness. As you expand spiritually, the connection between your self-identity and your Higher Self becomes closer and more pure than ever before. My energies reassure you of this process so that you can take steps forward to bring about its completion within you. If you find that you have reached a certain plateau in your growth and there is a sense of fear about moving to another level of under-

standing, I can give you reassurance and trust so that the Unknown is not traumatic. When you can replace your fear of the unknown with Unconditional Love, the flow of life-force energy into your body is increased. You must initiate action to understand the Spiritual Dimension of all physical reality. Once you make that commitment, I can lay the groundwork in your subtle bodies for your spiritual expansion.

Spiritual Aspects

Soul Tone: E

Chakra Affinities: Thymus Gland (1), Solar Plexus (1)

Subtle Body Affinities: Spiritual, Etheric, Emotional/Mental

Energy Focus: Spiritual Expansion

Element: Air

Cocreating with Moss Agate

Moss agate can be a bridge for connecting with your Higher Self and the Kingdoms of Nature, because it can increase the flow of Unconditional Love into your subtle bodies. It can be placed on the solar plexus or thymus gland to aid you in receiving additional life-force energies for healing and well-being. The essence can be taken before a meditation or a walk in the woods, to prepare you and help you release fears of the unknown. You can also try moss agate when you are working to heal your "inner child." The spiritual opening it gives can allow for the infusion of Unconditional Love, which in turn strengthens your self-identity and connection with your Higher Self.

Affirmation

"I find the God/Goddess/All That Is in all of life."

Obsidian

Physical Aspects

Obsidian is formed when silica-rich volcanic magma flows onto the Earth's surface and rapidly solidifies into an amorphous glassy solid. It is generally black, although sometimes it is mixed with brown and called mahogany obsidian, or white, which we call snowflake obsidian. As a natural glass, obsidian has a hardness of 5–5 1/2. We have utilized snowflake and mahogany obsidian.

The Obsidian Deva

My purpose is to uproot those energies from within your being that you no longer need. I am well suited to do this kind of work with the Human Kingdom because I am created through volcanic activity. When I have completed my work with you, there may be a heightened sense of vulnerability inside. You may experience a void in the space where imbalanced energies have been removed. Whatever sensations you may experience during my work, be reassured that the process you have undergone will allow more light to be present within. Sometimes you may experience flashbacks from your experience with me. Know, however, that if they do happen, they will be temporary in nature. When greater opportunities for spiritual growth of the Soul are present in your conscious awareness, then my purpose in your life is complete.

Spiritual Aspects

Soul Tone: Mahogany obsidian, C, snowflake obsidian, C#
Chakra Affinities: Root (1), Lower Abdomen (1), Solar Plexus (2)
Subtle Body Affinities: Emotional/Mental, Etheric, Spiritual
Energy Focus: Clearing
Element: Fire

Cocreating with Obsidian

The different kinds of obsidian have varying intensities, and we have found the snowflake and mahogany obsidians to provide more continuity in energy flow. Obsidian performs a task similar to dream imagery. In a dream the characters may at times exaggerate self-effacement, stubbornness, anger, etc. Your subconscious may paint these ludicrous pictures in order to attract your attention to the problem at hand. Obsidian can also amplify our negative emotions and thoughts so that we are more aware of them. Meditating on volcanoes will give you a feel for how obsidian may work with your energies. If you tend toward cynicism or rebelliousness on a particular subject, obsidian can abruptly cut through a hard outer shell. It can also be useful in a situation where you have been stubbornly fighting the process of looking within. Obsidian also helps release anger and can activate a positive sense of power that moves you to take charge of your situation. Obsidian can also be utilized to release subconscious memories that affect the lower three chakras.

Working with obsidian can have an irritating effect on your energy fields, so it is wise to be certain that obsidian is the mineral you need at a given time. It is best to work with the volcanic energies of obsidian with focused thoughts. Questions you might ask are: "What attitudes about myself do I need to change?" or "What attitudes or experiences do I need to be aware of in order to clear them?" Once you have become more aware, change your focus to "What qualities do I need to affirm in myself?"

Affirmation

"LETTING GO OF MY RESISTANCE TO LOOKING INWARD FREES MY
PERSONAL POWER TO BRING ABOUT CHANGE."

Opal

Physical Aspects

Opal is a hydrous silicon dioxide with a hardness of 5 1/2–6 1/2. There are three main groupings of opal: precious opal, fire opal, and common opal. Precious opal ranges from transparent to translucent and has a rainbow-like iridescence that changes as you look at it from different angles. Originally, opal was classified in the amorphous category of crystalline structures, and the iridescence was thought to be due to the refraction of light on its thin surface layers. In the 1960s, observations with an electron microscope revealed that opal is a very orderly structure of tiny spheres of the mineral cristobalite, layered in siliceous "jelly." The distance between these spheres is approximately the same length as the wavelength of light, so that diffraction occurs when the light hits the stone, causing the iridescence.

Sometimes opal is cut very thin and mounted as a doublet on another backing in order to bring out the colors. Opal has also been made synthetically, and there are several ways of livening up the color with artificial resins and dyes. Precious opal is classified as white or black opal, depending on whether the color flashes are in a white or dark background.

Opal contains water, and sometimes when it loses water, the opalescence diminishes. It can be restored by storing it in damp cotton wool.

Fire opal is named for its reddish-orange color. It does not have the rainbow iridescence and can be transparent or translucent. Glass imitations are on the market. Mexico is an excellent source for gem-quality fire opals.

White opal is mostly opaque and is also without the play of color. It looks like milky quartz but is softer and breaks differently. It is formed at a lower temperature than quartz and develops in a wide variety of rocks as a cavity filling. Common opal is widespread and easily obtainable.

The most well-known precious opal deposits are in Australia, Brazil, Japan, and the western United States. We have worked with the inexpensive common opal and the precious opal.

The Opal Deva

I am a bold and dynamic disperser of Light, and I can clear beliefs that limit your freedom and independence. I sense the importance of starting fresh and I help you initiate new ways of thinking and a more spontaneous approach to life. Because of my internal structure, I have the ability to express from a broader spectrum of color frequencies. Like you, I do not wish to be "possessed." I encourage freedom at all levels and help you build your own unique and positive Light space. My energies unlock the creative channels within you that are a part of your unique contribution to others.

Spiritual Aspects
Soul Tone: A
Chakra Affinities: Third Eye (1)
Subtle Body Affinities: Emotional/Mental, Spiritual, Etheric

Energy Focus: Clearing, Building

Element: Fire

Cocreating with Opal

Opal, with its expanding intensity, encourages both freedom and independence. Its energy can feel like firecrackers on the Fourth of July, or like a sunburst of energy. Opal can help you answer the question, "What blocks me from fully expressing myself?" It is a good stone for expanding creativity. Opal can also help you release anger and claim your self-worth. Opal also aids in locating and dissolving past-life memories.

Affirmation

"I AM NOW FREE AND INDEPENDENT, AS I EXPAND BEYOND PERCEIVED LIMITATIONS FROM MY PAST."

Pearl

Physical Aspects

Pearls are not classified as minerals because they are organic in origin. They are formed by two particular species of shellfish called pearl mollusks and pearl oysters as an immune defense against irritants such as parasites. When a parasite enters the fleshy part of the mollusk, the animal surrounds it with a secreted substance called mother-of-pearl or nacre. Mother-of-pearl is calcium carbonate (84–92 percent) cemented together with an organic substance called conchiolin (4–13 percent). Mother-of-pearl can be pink, silver, cream, golden, green, or blue. It is the substance produced by the mantle of the mollusk that lines its inner shell.

The finest natural pearls are called oriental pearls, and they come from the Persian Gulf, off the coast of southern India, and Australia. Freshwater pearls are found in the rivers of the Mississippi Valley.

The increased demand for pearls has led to their cultivation, particularly in Japan. Today, cultured pearls make up about 90 percent of the total trade. Cultured pearls are made by inserting a rounded mother-of-pearl bead, along with a piece of tissue from the mantle of a pearl mollusk, into another pearl mollusk. Natural pearls and cultured pearl are very similar in appearance, and cultured pearls must be designated as such.

We have worked with mother-of-pearl, in the form of a small polished stone, which comes from the mantle or inner lining of the shell.

The Pearl Deva

My energies gently encourage you to look at those things that are upsetting you emotionally. Sometimes your emotions need to be agitated to help you see what you need to release. My work is best done with those whose sensitivity to their emotional nature is finely tuned. Although I can help you access past lives, I am best utilized in helping you release and balance the experiences of this present life.

Many of you live life constantly surrounded by a protective outer shell that you have created. Sometimes you need the nurturing of emotional detachment from a situation. Sometimes you need to risk yourself in a situation that feels like a sacrifice in order to be able to receive at a later time. The sacrifice is that of becoming more vulnerable and sensitive to your outer world. You acquire wisdom in learning to move back and forth from emotional detachment and emotional risk.

My physical function as a protector shows one side of reality, and my spiritual quality as a catalyst to encourage emotional risk shows another side. In each way I serve a teaching function, so that you have a complete picture. When you can integrate emotional protection with vulnerability, you will have balance.

Spiritual Aspects
Soul Tone: A
Chakra Affinities: Third Eye (1), Heart (2)
Subtle Body Affinities: Emotional/Mental, Spiritual, Etheric
Energy Focus: Clearing
Element: Water

Cocreating with Pearl

Once you have started a release process of some kind, pearl brings a sense of inner strength, emotional peace, and a nurturing space for you to complete your work. Pearl essence can be helpful in a personal or counseling situation to encourage emotional risk. You can work with it also for emotional protection.

Affirmation

"As I risk myself emotionally in order to heal, I am protected and nurtured."

Peridot

Physical Aspects

Peridot, or olivine, as it is sometimes called, is a transparent, yellow-green magnesium iron silicate. Its unique green is due to the iron and traces of nickel in its content. Peridot's hardness is 6 1/2–7 and it has an orthorhombic crystalline structure. The most well-known deposit is on St. John's Island on the Red Sea, where it has been mined for 3,500 years. Peridot is also found in Burma, South Africa, Brazil, Mexico, and Arizona.

The Peridot Deva

Jade says happiness is a state of being. *I say that happiness is an* expression of being. *My purpose is to give you joy, so that you can spontaneously spread my Light to all other lifestreams. When you are feeling "joy-full" and sunny, you can see the sun in others. I encourage you to keep the life-force energies flowing by expressing your delight. Take time to give to others, and tell them how much you appreciate their work and their gifts of service.*

Spiritual Aspects

Soul Tone: E

Chakra Affinities: Heart (1), Solar Plexus (1)

Subtle Body Affinities: Emotional/Mental, Spiritual, Etheric

Energy Focus: Building
Element: Fire

Cocreating with Peridot

Peridot revitalizes the sense of inner joy that shines like the sun. It encourages you to express that joy to others. Peridot opens you to giving and receiving. When you dislike certain aspects of your daily life, peridot can give you an optimism that helps you delight in little things. Peridot also encourages an extroverted expression of appreciation of others in order to keep you from taking others for granted. It helps you feel a confident joy that you have something to give, and reminds you how beautiful you are and how beautiful the world is.

Affirmation

"INNER JOY LIGHTS MY WAY, AND I SHARE THAT JOY WITH OTHERS."

Pyrite

Physical Aspects

Pyrite is the stone that is commonly called "fool's gold." It is an iron disulphide with a hardness of 6–6 1/2 and an isometric crystalline structure. The crystals occur predominantly in cubes but can assume other geometric shapes as well. Pyrite is the most widespread and abundant of the sulphide minerals and can be found in a number of places in the United States. Pyrites that can be cut are mined in Italy.

The Pyrite Deva

My energies help provide a base of life-force energies that can be utilized throughout your physical vehicle. I see myself as an energy channel, because I function as a transmitter of life-force energies that are continually being received from the sun and the core energy of Planet Earth herself. Inertia takes place when there is insufficient energy present to generate movement. This can occur at any level of your being. I often hear lifestreams express, *"I really don't want to think about this,"* or *"I am too tired and worn out to make a change." Yes, I see an emotional and mental aspect to this situation. However, I work by adding greater life-force energy to the system. The integration of additional life-force energy and a change in thinking is a key for the return of normal energy flow.*

Spiritual Aspects

Soul Tone: C

Chakra Affinities: Root (1), Base of Spine (1)

Subtle Body Affinities: All

Energy Focus: Building

Element: Fire

Cocreating with Pyrite

Pyrite does not give specific emotional or mental qualities. Rather, it is a more generalized energy builder, as clear quartz crystal can be. When you need energy on any level, place pyrite at the root or base of the spine and affirm that you are receiving an energy boost. You can follow pyrite with other stones, which may then have a more powerful effect because they will have more energy to realign. If you take the essence you may feel a more diffused, overall "spread" of energy that can revitalize you on whatever level you need.

Affirmation

"I OPEN TO RECEIVE ADDITIONAL LIFE-FORCE ENERGY WHEREVER IT IS NEEDED."

Rhodochrosite

Physical Aspects

Rhodochrosite is an opaque manganese carbonate that is concentrically banded in layers of rose and white. It has a hardness of 4 and belongs to the trigonal system. There are several large deposits in Argentina, as well as in Romania and Colorado.

The Rhodochrosite Deva

I teach you about loving yourself unconditionally. When you find it difficult to forgive and accept yourself and others, you can feel lonely and separated from the life-force energies of Unconditional Love. I help you to develop a compassionate heart. I do not mean a "bleeding heart," where you take the burdens of others upon yourself. Rather, it is listening to yourself and others with sensitive ears and letting your responses be channeled with Unconditional Purity and Love.

My energies work effectively for the release of pain and deep hurt that you may have stored within your heart. Self-acceptance releases pain. Mistakes really are gifts that allow us to bring ourselves in alignment with Divine Harmony. Always focus on the beauty of who you are, rather than the imperfection of what you are not.

Spiritual Aspects

Soul Tone: F

Chakra Affinities: Heart (1), Solar Plexus (2)

Subtle Body Affinities: Emotional/Mental, Etheric, Spiritual

Energy Focus: Clearing, Building

Element: Fire/Water

Cocreating with Rhodochrosite

Renewal is a key quality for rhodochrosite. There is a fiery intensity that strengthens the initiative to begin again after pain. There is also a watery, gentler compassion that brings self-acceptance. Rhodochrosite can help ease the loneliness that comes from feeling "not good enough." As a heart opener, rhodochrosite can dissolve anger and self-criticism; therefore, it is a catalyst for forgiveness of self and others.

Affirmation

"I ACCEPT THAT I AM TRULY A LOVABLE BEING, AND I FORGIVE THOSE WHO HAVE FORGOTTEN THAT THEY ARE LOVED."

Rhodonite

Physical Aspects

Rhodonite ranges from a light rose to flesh-pink stone with black veins and inclusions of manganese oxide. It is a manganese silicate with a hardness of 5 1/2–6 1/2 and a triclinic crystalline structure. Rhodonite forms in metamorphic rocks and is mined in Sweden, Australia, the United States, and Canada.

The Rhodonite Deva

Sometimes I sense within you a deep longing to keep the past. When you hold onto possessions or memories of the past, you draw comparisons with the present. You develop expectations that seem to fall short of what you enjoyed "back then," and you experience only fleeting happiness. My energies help you allow the past to rest as a treasured memory, without a need to resurrect it in the present moment. Whenever you have to release something on the Earth Plane, there is often a sense of loss, and I bring you a sense of empathy and healing. I help you understand that you cannot live through your past while seeking to grow in the present.

Spiritual Aspects

Soul Tone: D#

Chakra Affinities: Lower Abdomen (1), Solar Plexus (1)

Subtle Body Affinities: Emotional/Mental, Etheric

Energy Focus: Clearing

Element: Water/Earth

Cocreating with Rhodonite

Rhodonite encourages you to get on with your daily life and forget looking back at the past. Therefore, it is useful when you get caught in nostalgic memories and cloud the present with unrealistic expectations or lack of focus. Rhodonite helps you release your hold on what was and accept what is in the present. It can heighten an interest in daily affairs.

Affirmation

"I RELEASE MY LONGING FOR THE PAST AS I FIND IN EVERY DAY
SOMETHING BEAUTIFUL AND NEW FOR ME TO APPRECIATE."

Rose Quartz

Physical Aspects

Rose quartz is a translucent pink silicon dioxide with a hardness of 7
and a trigonal crystalline structure. The rose color comes from the trace
mineral titanium. Crystals with flat faces are rare and have only been found
within the past few years. Brazil and the Malagasy Republic have large
deposits of rose quartz.

The Rose Quartz Deva

*I help you to live this life as fully as you can, and to find
pleasure in all of life around you. I also help you to move from a
place of being hard-hearted to a gentle place of being more "flex-
ible-hearted." I fooled you. You thought I was going to say "softhearted." Some people think that to be softhearted is to be weak.
To me being softhearted is to learn about the power of your
emotions and how your emotions can create a positive flow of
life-force energy. When you are enjoying beauty, the flow of soft-
ness and delight in your heart creates a positive energy of Unconditional Love in yourself and others.*

Spiritual Aspects

Soul Tone: F
Chakra Affinities: Heart (1)
Subtle Body Affinities: Emotional/Mental, Etheric, Spiritual
Energy Focus: Building
Element: Water

Cocreating with Rose Quartz

Rose quartz builds self-confidence and self-acceptance by asking you
to give pleasure to yourself and to smile. It encourages you to slow down,

be more light-hearted, and make time in your life for joy and delight. Rose quartz can also heighten your awareness of the beauty around you in order to dissolve gloom, despondency, and over-seriousness.

Affirmation

"I DELIGHT IN PLAY AND PLEASURE."

Ruby

Physical Aspects

Ruby is the trade name for red corundum. It is an aluminum oxide with a hardness of 9 and a trigonal crystalline structure. Ruby can range in color from rose to a dark purplish red. It gets color from traces of chrome. As a rough stone, ruby looks dull, but when cut, its luster is like diamond. Inclusions of rutile in a cut ruby can look like a six-pointed star; this is called star ruby. Because ruby is comparatively heavy, it is mined by panning and then picking out the rubies by hand. Important deposits are in Burma and Sri Lanka. Rubies are also found in North Carolina. There are many imitations on the market in the form of doublets, triplets, and synthetic rubies.

The Ruby Deva

My guiding purpose is to help you evolve into a greater expression of spiritual nature. When you are being your true Divine Essence, you are in a space to give Unconditional Love to others, as well as to Nature. It takes courage to refrain from judging another lifestream and to follow your intuitive sensitivity rather than your logical mind. It takes courage to take on the role of leadership when others have become disconnected from the group focus. My energies can strengthen you in these kinds of experiences, so that the expression of your will is purified through the Unconditional Love of your heart. As you radiate this state of being, know that you are creating positive life-force energies for the personal and spiritual growth of others.

Spiritual Aspects

Soul Tone: F# (lighter rubies may test F, darker rubies may test F#)

Chakra Affinities: Heart (1), Root (1)

Subtle Body Affinities: Emotional/Mental, Spiritual, Etheric

Energy Focus: Building

Element: Fire

Cocreating with Ruby

Ruby's fiery energy builds confidence by strengthening your courage and will to be who you are. It is helpful against self-dislike and can give you an energy boost when you are doing something you have never done before. When you need to move into a leadership role, ruby can give you the confidence to make decisions that others may not like. Ruby's intensity will keep you moving in your chosen direction with a strong, bright light.

Affirmation

"I HAVE THE COURAGE AND STRENGTH TO BE WHO I TRULY AM."

Rutilated Quartz

Physical Aspects

Rutilated quartz is clear quartz with needles of brown rutile or titanium dioxide scattered throughout. The mineral futile is slightly less hard at 6–6 1/2 than quartz and is of igneous and metamorphic origin. The rutile needles can vary in color due to the heat exposure they receive during the solidification process in quartz. Rutilated quartz can be found all over the world.

The Rutilated Quartz Deva

With my deep and penetrating energy, I seek areas within your being where you need to "get to the core of the matter" and release imbalanced thought patterns that have outlived their usefulness. I maintain a sustained intensity of focused light so that you can more clearly see the thoughts you need to release.

You may have wondered if it is possible to program my species, and the answer is yes indeed. An ideal program would utilize the energy capacities of both quartz and rutile. You are encouraged to experiment with this in your own practice.

Because I am a catalyst to bring greater clarity and understanding to your life experiences, I can reorder and balance an area after clearing has taken place. This is particularly true if the amounts of quartz and rutile are roughly equal in the stone.

Greater conscious expansion is occurring on the spiritual levels of your being. The quality of life-force energies that you receive into your energy field is being continuously refined to support you in your chosen service on the Planet in this present lifetime.

Spiritual Aspects
Soul Tone: All tones

Chakra Affinities: All Chakras

Subtle Body Affinities: All Bodies

Energy Focus: Clearing

Element: Fire

Cocreating with Rutilated Quartz
Rutilated quartz will clear at the level or levels where the need is greatest, and that is where you will feel its action most strongly. As an essence, rutilated quartz can sometimes relieve minor pain such as headaches. Emotionally and mentally, rutilated quartz has an incisive quality that can be utilized to release troubled thoughts and feelings after a trying day, or before going to bed. It can be helpful when you are working on chronic habitual thought patterns. If you are feeling overly vulnerable as you begin working with rutilated quartz, you can focus on the clarity of quartz filling you with protective, expanding light. Rutilated quartz can give a sense of clarity and freedom, and it is very versatile as an emergency tension releaser.

Affirmation

"I CAN NOW SEE CLEARLY BEYOND THE ILLUSIONS OF MY PAST."

Sapphire

Physical Aspects

Sapphire, like ruby, belongs to the corundum family and occurs in blue, clear, pink, orange, yellow, green, purple, and black. Red corundum is called ruby, as we have stated earlier. Sapphire is an aluminum oxide with a hardness of 9, and it belongs to the trigonal system. Blue sapphire gets its coloring from iron and titanium. The other colors are due to varying amounts of these minerals as well as chrome and vanadium.

The main sapphire-bearing rocks are marble, basalt, and pegmatite. Mining is a simple, labor-intensive process. Gravel from hand-dug holes is panned with water and searched by hand. Most of the gem-quality sapphires come from the Orient in Burma, Thailand, India, and Sri Lanka. Light blue sapphires are found in Montana. Clear sapphire is a trade name for pure corundum. We will discuss the clear and light blue sapphires from Montana.

Clear Sapphire Deva

My energies deepen your inner faith, so that in any circumstance you can reassure yourself that all is well. You express the quality of faith when you stand alone with commitment to your spiritual purpose. Faith is built internally and the quality of faith is also transmitted to you from the spirit world. Through me you can learn that the practice of optimistic faith and trust brings healing.

It is also faith that inspires you to reach toward a greater expansion of Light. As you overcome your doubts and trust the process of your spiritual growth, you may sense your crown chakra opening. This opening is a vital first step to exploring other spiritual dimensions.

Clear Sapphire—Spiritual Aspects

Soul Tone: A#

Chakra Affinities: Crown (1), Third Eye (1)

Subtle Body Affinities: Emotional/Mental, Spiritual, Etheric

Energy Focus: Clearing, Building

Element: Fire/Air

Cocreating with Clear Sapphire

Clear sapphire can aid you in gently releasing unneeded, imbalanced energy so that you can continue to grow and heal. If, for example, you have a health problem for which medical answers are unsatisfactory, clear sapphire can open your awareness to the possibilities of spiritual healing. If you or a client are new to particular concepts of spiritual energy and higher spiritual awareness, clear sapphire inspires reassurance and a strong sense of the presence of Light and Love.

Clear Sapphire Affirmation

"I HAVE FAITH AND TRUST IN THE PROCESS OF MY GROWTH TOWARD THE LIGHT."

Blue Sapphire Deva

When you seek to expand spiritually, you may need to be nurtured and supported in your practice of faith. I fill you with a compassionate, eternal peace that creates a calm environment for you to expand your spiritual sensitivities.

Blue Sapphire—Spiritual Aspects

Soul Tone: A

Chakra Affinities: Third Eye (1)

Subtle Body Affinities: Emotional/Mental, Spiritual, Etheric

Energy Focus: Clearing, Building

Element: Fire/Air

Cocreating with Blue Sapphire

When there has been emotional pain and trauma, the inspiring and peaceful qualities of blue sapphire can move you from feeling encumbered to feeling free. Blue sapphire can strengthen your faith, so that you can release self-judgment and move into a healing space of Unconditional Love.

Blue Sapphire Affirmation

"KNOWING THAT I AM ACTIVELY GUIDED AND SUPPORTED IN MY GROWTH TOWARD THE LIGHT BRINGS ME PEACE."

Selenite

Physical Aspects

Selenite is the clear variety of gypsum. It is a very soft hydrous calcium sulfate with a hardness of 1 1/2–2 and a monoclinic crystalline structure. Selenite crystals are often rather flat and rhombic in shape. Gypsum is a common sulphate mineral that develops principally in sedimentary rocks. Good crystals are found in Mexico and the United States. Selenite is not considered a gemstone because it is too soft and sensitive to cut for jewelry, but like other minerals, it has a place in healing. We work with the clear and cloudy white selenite.

The Selenite Deva

My energies can help you access the Spirit Guides that support you on your life path, for I wish to reassure you that you are not alone in this life. If you wish to know your Spirit Guides, work with me in a meditative, receptive state and visualize yourself surrounded by pure White Light. Affirm in your thoughts the desire to know the essence of the Spirit Guides that are near you. I encourage you to ask, "What is your purpose for being in a dialogue with me?" Your Guides come not to change you, but to support you in your growth.

Your Guides are Spirit Beings who have been on the Earth Plane and choose to continue their service in the area in which they worked while on the Earth. This is not usually done until additional knowledge and awareness has been assimilated. They match their expertise to a lifestream such as yourself that is following a similar path on the Earth. First, the Spirit Being mentally approaches the lifestream and observes the energy pattern. If the energy pattern becomes discordant, then the Spirit Being discontinues contact for a period of time. If further contact is desired by the lifestream, then the Spirit Guide initiates that contact through the crown center of the lifestream. Once the foundation has been set for communication, the process can be refined and expanded. I say, open yourself to the world of Spirit to help you understand and work through your Earth Plane experiences.

Spiritual Aspects

Soul Tone: A#, A, depending on the individual stone.

Chakra Affinities: Crown (1), Third Eye (1)

Subtle Body Affinities: Spiritual

Energy Focus: Spiritual Expansion

Element: Air

Cocreating with Selenite

Selenite is a gentle crown and third eye-opener. Work with the stone when you wish to contact your Spirit Guides. Individual selenite stones seem to vary more in their individual frequencies than some others. Chakra affinity and compatibility with other stones needs to be checked with each individual selenite.

Affirmation

"I AFFIRM MY CONNECTION WITH MY SPIRIT GUIDES."

Smoky Quartz

Physical Aspects

Smoky quartz is a pale brown to black silicon dioxide with a hardness of 7 and a trigonal crystalline structure. It is frequently found with inclusions of rutile. Sometimes it is heat-treated to make the color lighter. Smoky quartz is found in Brazil, Switzerland, Colorado, and New Hampshire.

Smoky Quartz Deva

I give you a sense of emotional security that allows you to be open to new experiences. I reassure you that you will not fail in your new endeavors. I remind you that it is not important whether you win or lose. What is important is that you learn and let your experiences give you understanding that will be helpful to you later.

Spiritual Aspects

Soul Tone: C

Chakra Affinities: Root (1), Lower Abdomen (2), Solar Plexus (2)

Subtle Body Affinities: Emotional/Mental, Etheric, Spiritual

Energy Focus: Building

Element: Water

Cocreating With Smoky Quartz

Smoky quartz stabilizes the emotions and can reassure you on an ongoing basis whenever you fear failure. It also encourages you to experience new things and develop an attitude of self-acceptance in the learning process.

Affirmation

"I FIND SECURITY IN KNOWING THAT I CAN LEARN, WHETHER I WIN OR LOSE."

Sodalite

Physical Aspects

Sodalite is similar in appearance to lapis lazuli, except that it is often a deeper, more striking indigo blue. It is a sodium aluminum silicate with chlorine and has a hardness of 5 1/2–6 and an isometric crystalline structure. The larger deposits are in Canada and Brazil, and it is also found in the United States.

The Sodalite Deva

I help to bring order and calmness, primarily at your mental level, but extending to what you verbally express. Focus goes hand in hand with order, and mental focus is achieved when you can slow and still your mind of incessant chatter. When your mind is ordered, then there is no wasted energy through the impulsive expression of irrelevant thoughts. I help you to think clearly and say what you mean. When your conscious mind is still, you will know whether the guidance you are receiving is coming from your Higher Guidance or from some other part of you. Effortless choices are made in a state of calm, ordered peace.

Spiritual Aspects

Soul Tone: A, A#

Chakra Affinities: Third Eye (1)

Subtle Body Affinities: Mental, Spiritual, Etheric

Energy Focus: Building

Element: Air/Earth

Cocreating with Sodalite

When a fan is running, the blades look like an undifferentiated mass, but when the motor is slowed down or turned off, the noise level drops and you can see the individual blades. Sodalite is like the fan motor. It aids the conscious mind through slowing down and stilling it, so that you can identify and clarify the key mental points. Therefore it is helpful if you have a tendency to mental panic when fearful, or if you are indecisive at times.

It can be helpful to take sodalite essence before you begin to meditate, or to hold the stone during meditation. Sodalite calms and stills the chattering conscious mind so that you can achieve a single-pointed focus more easily. Sodalite aids concentration and mental discipline, so that your mind doesn't wander off the subject.

Affirmation

"MY MIND IS CALM AND ORDERED, SO THAT I CAN CONCENTRATE WITH A SINGULAR FOCUS."

Spinel (Red)

Physical Aspects

Although spinel comes in red, blue, violet, and brown, it is the red spinel that is most often seen in the gem trade. Red spinel has often been confused with ruby, because they are similar in hardness and brilliance. Spinel is a magnesium aluminum oxide with a hardness of 8 and an isometric crystalline structure. Similar to ruby it gets its red color from traces of chromium. Spinel crystallizes in an octahedral shape and forms in plutonic and metamorphic rocks. Spinel is easily manufactured: yellow, green, and clear spinels are usually synthetic. Blue spinel is widely used as a substitute for aquamarine. Spinel is found chiefly in the gem gravels of Sri Lanka, Burma, and Thailand. It is also found in Brazil and the United States. We have worked with the red spinel.

The Red Spinel Deva

I can help you reconnect with the power that is you. When you seek recognition and approval from others, then you create meaning for your life that is dependent on the beliefs and love of others. If you deny aspects of your being that are truly a unique part of your self-expression, you may lack enjoyment in life, or not feel connected to your creative tasks. I help you recognize and affirm your inner self, so that you can truly live, instead of merely existing according to patterns set by others. When you feel that your life may be meaningless, I can connect you with feelings you have hidden, or gifts you have not expressed. If your life has meaning, and you have inner recognition of Self, then you will have the inner drive in all circumstances to complete what you start. Completion of your tasks is its own fulfillment, and your sense of who you are is strengthened.

Spiritual Aspects

Soul Tone: E

Chakra Affinities: Solar Plexus (1)

Subtle Body Affinities: Emotional/Mental

Energy Focus: Clearing

Element: Fire

Cocreating with Red Spinel

Red spinel affirms your resourcefulness when you are holding back from committing yourself to a project or service. It diminishes timidity and reluctance and increases willingness and confidence when you are dealing with beliefs about not being good enough. It helps dissolve self-judgment and criticism and affirms inner recognition. Red spinel, with its fiery energy, inspires you to finish projects you have started.

Affirmation

"I AM RESOURCEFUL AND CAPABLE OF FINISHING WHAT I START."

Sugilite

Physical Aspects

Sugilite is a uniquely colored reddish-violet stone that has been described as looking like grape jelly. It is a potassium ferric lithium silicate with a hardness of 6–6 1/2 and a hexagonal crystalline structure. The trace mineral manganese gives the pink-lavender color. Although it was discovered in Japan in 1944, cuttable sugilite was not known until 1975, when a gem-quality deposit was found in South Africa. Other deposits are located in India. You may also find sugilite referred to as royal luvulite, royal azel, and cybeline.

The Sugilite Deva

Whenever you make reference to what separates you from others through imbalanced thoughts and feelings, my energies reaffirm your true Divine Nature as Unconditional Love. If you are suffering from physical imbalance, I say to you that at this time you are choosing the physical vehicle as the optimal way in which to learn about self-acceptance and Unconditional Love. Whenever you are feeling judgmental toward yourself, my energies can help you to see the Light within you that is eternally connected to the Divine Source. Accept and value yourself as you truly are, and an enduring healing on all levels will take place.

Spiritual Aspects

Soul Tone: A#

Chakra Affinities: Third Eye (1), Crown (2)

Subtle Body Affinities: Spiritual, Emotional/Mental

Energy Focus: Building, Clearing

Element: Water

Cocreating with Sugilite

Sugilite teaches a lesson that is sometimes very hard to grasp at the gut level: we are truly manifestations of Unconditional Love. Sugilite is very flowing and self-affirming, and through its energies we can understand that we are like angels in physical form; we are precious Divine Beings. When you are working with a physical imbalance, meditate with sugilite to help you dialogue with the specific body part in question and to understand what you need to affirm. Then you can visualize yourself as already whole and perfectly healthy. Sugilite can also aid in dissolving overly judgmental attitudes toward yourself and others that may keep you feeling separate.

Affirmation

"I AM A DIVINE MANIFESTATION OF LOVE."

Sunstone (Orange)

Physical Aspects

Orange sunstone is a sodium, calcium, aluminum, silicate member of the feldspar family and is also called aventurine feldspar or oligoclase. Its coloring is orange-brown with a metallic glitter. Orange sunstone has a hardness of 6–6 1/2 and a triclinic crystalline structure. Sunstone can be found in the United States, India, Canada, South Norway, and Russia. *For information on yellow sunstone, see yellow orthoclase feldspar.*

Orange Sunstone Deva

I help you to grow from any fears that you may have related to the expansion of self. When you can repeatedly see yourself as a vibrant, vital, confident being, this pattern becomes impressed as a thought form into the subconscious mind. I work with your physical body, giving you a sense of expansion and vitality at that level. As a catalyst in your expansion on the emotional and mental levels, I tell you that you are now greater than you have ever been, and send you impressions of this way of perceiving yourself. You determine the degree of expansion that you are willing to accept. In truth you are a limitless being, with many opportunities to bring greater Light to your physical body and your physical world.

Spiritual Aspects
Soul Tone: D#
Chakra Affinities: Root (1), Lower Abdomen (1)
Subtle Body Affinities: Etheric, Emotional/Mental, Spiritual
Energy Focus: Building
Element: Water

Cocreating with Orange Sunstone
Orange sunstone has a sunny vitality and an expansiveness that can get you moving again if you have limited your possibilities in life. It gently and lovingly encourages you not to take life's setbacks to heart and to *think big*. Explore and expand your possibilities and know that the sky is the limit.

Affirmation
"THERE IS NO LIMIT TO WHAT I CAN DO."

Tiger's Eye

Physical Aspects

Tiger's eye is a brown quartz silicon dioxide with lustrous yellow and brown parallel fibers. It has a hardness of 7 and belongs to the trigonal system. The yellow-gold colors are due to iron oxides. Tiger's eye has the property of chatoyancy, which means that it glimmers with a small ray of light on the surface, like the eyes of a cat. The largest deposits of tiger's eye are in South Africa, Australia, Burma, India, and the United States.

The Tiger's Eye Deva

Your personal will and the emotions that accompany it are intricately related to the proper use of power. When your will is in harmony with your Higher Will, your self-confidence is maximally enhanced. I help you act wisely in your everyday life and I keep your feet firmly planted on the ground. True power is built patiently from small steps. Each step is an act of will that is in harmony with your intuitive sense of rightness and accomplished with perseverance.

Spiritual Aspects

Soul Tone: C#

Chakra Affinities: Root (1), Solar Plexus (1), Lower Abdomen (1)

Subtle Body Affinities: Etheric, Emotional/Mental

Energy Focus: Building

Element: Earth/Fire

Cocreating with Tiger's Eye

When you feel as though your daily activities are not getting you anywhere, tiger's eye teaches you to affirm a purpose to your activities. Perhaps you are building endurance and patience. The foundation of a house lies mostly underground and must be carefully laid out and very well built. Affirm that your activities are building a foundation of self-reliance, which then becomes your personal power.

Affirmation

"My personal power comes from my belief in my purpose and my strength."

Topaz

Physical Aspects

The most popular color of topaz is yellow, and in antiquity all yellow stones were called topaz. The term "precious topaz" is used today to refer to an aluminum fluorosilicate that comes in clear, blue, yellow, and pink colors. It is formed under the influence of fluorine and water during the formation of granite pegmatites. Topaz has a hardness of 8 and an orthorhombic crystalline structure. It has a perfect cleavage, so care must be taken in cutting. Russia is a source for gem-quality blue topaz, and Brazil is well-known for its clear and yellow topaz. Other deposits are located in Sri Lanka, Burma, and the United States. Sometimes citrine and heat-treated amethysts are sold as "gold topaz" or "Madeira topaz." True topaz is often called "precious topaz," as we stated earlier. Yellow topaz is also often referred to as "imperial topaz." Sometimes the clear variety is irradiated to make a sky blue color.

We will first discuss clear topaz, and then move to yellow and blue topaz.

The Clear Topaz Deva

My purpose is to inspire the expansion of your mental and intuitive faculties. I broaden your comprehension of spiritual truth. You must decide whether a particular understanding can be connected with other beliefs so that a continuity is established. If not, then I say "travel light." Do not weigh down your existence with a disordered mind. As I expand the channel of Light that connects you with your Higher Self, seek the oneness, joy, and beauty that is part of all spiritual truth.

Clear Topaz—Spiritual Aspects

Soul Tone: A#

Chakra Affinities: Third Eye (1), Crown (2)

Subtle Body Affinities: Spiritual, Mental, Etheric

Energy Focus: Building
Element: Air

Cocreating with Clear Topaz

Clear topaz aids in the birth of new understanding. With its joyful, active, uplifting energies, it can help you change knowledge to wisdom. Working with topaz is like reading a book about personal growth or spiritual wisdom and having an "aha" experience. You suddenly "get" what the author is trying to say. Utilize clear topaz whenever you are reading or studying, in order to assimilate new spiritual wisdom. Topaz keeps you from being discouraged when you don't understand something. Also, when you wish to better understand what you are to learn from a recent experience, try working with clear topaz.

Clear Topaz Affirmation

"I JOYFULLY EXPAND THE HORIZONS OF MY SPIRITUAL UNDERSTANDING."

The Yellow Topaz Deva

Like clear topaz, my energies can help to expand the higher creative capacities of your mind. As your conscious awareness becomes more elevated, you see life from a broader viewpoint. That viewpoint then needs to be implemented in your physical world. My energies contain two specific qualities that foster this process within you. First, I can give an inherent recognition that this new understanding has practical application. Second, my energies instill a desire to integrate this seed essence into a manifestation.

Yellow Topaz—Spiritual Aspects

Soul Tone: E
Chakra Affinities: Solar Plexus (1), Third Eye (1).
Subtle Body Affinities: Mental, Spiritual, Etheric
Energy Focus: Building
Element: Air

Cocreating with Yellow Topaz

Yellow topaz helps you to simplify the wisdom and understanding you receive, so that you can assimilate it in your conscious mind in a way that is conducive to practical application. Yellow topaz can stimulate innovative ideas for any project or research. Yellow topaz together with citrine is a wonderful combination for the student or researcher.

Yellow Topaz Affirmation

"I SEEK TO COMPREHEND THE PRACTICAL WISDOM IN ALL MY EXPERIENCE, AND I MANIFEST THAT WISDOM."

The Blue Topaz Deva

Many times when a lifestream has experienced expansion on the mental and spiritual levels, frustration and doubt surface, as comparisons are made with the present beliefs and attitudes about self. My energies bring you a sense of peace and reassurance. No one is saying that the experiences gained through mental and spiritual expansion are going to blend in perfectly with how you view life. Give yourself the permission and space to assimilate new understandings into your consciousness in a gentle, loving way. Remember that questioning the meaning of things is natural and acceptable. I tell you that the pure essence of your knowing is what will find its right space in your reality, however you perceive it to be.

Blue Topaz—Spiritual Aspects

Soul Tone: A

Chakra Affinities: Third Eye (1)

Subtle Body Affinities: Emotional/Mental, Spiritual, Etheric

Energy Focus: Building

Element: Air

Cocreating with Blue Topaz

Blue topaz works similarly to clear topaz, but its energies are calmer and more peaceful. Blue topaz can help you accept new ideas when you feel agitated by the discrepancies created in your belief systems. Blue topaz does not seem to combine as well with other stones as clear topaz.

Blue Topaz Affirmation

"I CALMLY ACCEPT THE IMPLICATIONS OF MY EXPANDING SPIRITUAL UNDERSTANDING."

Tourmaline

Physical Aspects

Similar to the quartz family, tourmalines come in a wide variety of colors and have been popular semi-precious gemstones. Tourmaline is a complex borosilicate with a hardness of 7 and a trigonal crystalline structure. In their rough form, tourmaline crystals are typically prismatic and heavily striated. When they are cut and polished, they can be easily confused with other stones of similar colors. You can see different color tints, depending on which direction the light is traveling through the crystal. This means that if a dark crystal is cut with its flat part or table parallel to the long axis, the color will be lightened. Conversely, a lighter tourmaline cut perpendicular to the long axis will appear deeper in color. Similar to quartz, tourmaline also has piezoelectric properties. By heating or cooling it, or applying a mechanical pressure, you can electrically charge a tourmaline so that one end becomes negative and the other becomes positive.

Tourmaline is a common stone in granite pegmatites, so their occurrence is widespread. In the United States, gem-quality tourmaline comes from Maine and California. Elsewhere, tourmaline is mined in the Urals in Russia, Sri Lanka, the Malagasy Republic, and Brazil.

The different colors of tourmaline have some varying properties. Therefore, the most common varieties for healing will be discussed separately. They include green, pink, watermelon, black, and blue tourmaline. *Black tourmalinated quartz is included under black tourmaline.*

Green Tourmaline—Physical Aspects

Green tourmaline, or elbaite, is the most common member of the tourmaline family. It gets its color from lithium, sodium, and potassium trace minerals. In fact, elbaite is sometimes called lithium tourmaline. The most valued color is an emerald green, and sometimes the darker green tourmaline is heated to approximately 1,000 degrees Fahrenheit to produce this green.

The Green Tourmaline Deva

Through my energies you can learn to be committed to your goals and at the same time be non-attached to the process and its outcome. Non-attachment means that you allow yourself to step aside from the creative form of your goal and allow it to grow and expand from the original focus. When there are disruptions in the flow you make adjustments to restimulate the flow so that your decisions come from the perspective of an overall direction. The steps you take to restimulate the flow also energize the thought form of the original goal. However, I also tell you that you do not need to worry about each little step along the way. You can trust that the flow is like a river, taking you where you want to go, even when you go through little backwater whirlpools or meandering sidestreams. You will find balance in letting go of your attachments to how your life needs to be.

Green Tourmaline—Spiritual Aspects

Soul Tone: E

Chakra Affinities: Solar Plexus (1), Lower Abdomen (1)

Subtle Body Affinities: Emotional/Mental, Etheric, Spiritual

Energy Focus: Building

Element: Water

Cocreating with Green Tourmaline

Green tourmaline gives emotional balance through helping you let go of expectations about how things should be. It helps you detach from a situation in a nonjudgmental way. Green tourmaline can calm anxiety as you go for job interviews or when your life takes an unexpected turn. If you find yourself worrying or saying "what if," as you prepare for an endeavor, green tourmaline will calm you. Green tourmaline has a way of balancing emotional highs and lows so that you can let whatever happens happen with more equanimity.

"Ask for what you want, but don't demand it.
Accept whatever happens for now.
Turn up your light even if you don't get what you want."
—Ken Keyes

Green Tourmaline Affirmation

"I LET GO OF MY INNER ATTACHMENTS ABOUT HOW MY LIFE NEEDS TO BE."

Pink Tourmaline—Physical Aspects

Pink tourmaline, or rubellite, ranges in color from pink to red. A ruby red is the most valued color of tourmaline in the gem trade. Red and pink tourmaline get their color from a combination of trace elements, including lithium, sodium, and potassium.

The Pink Tourmaline Deva

I teach you that Unconditional Love cannot be possessed or manipulated. My energies help you to clear your attachment about how love "should" be expressed in an experience, when your expectations become too high or too fixed, and the object of your devotion deviates from those expectations, I challenge you to let go of your expectations. I can also help you remain in a state of balance by teaching you to enjoy the flow of your life, wherever it takes you.

Pink Tourmaline—Spiritual Aspects

Soul Tone: D
Chakra Affinities: Lower Abdomen (1), Heart (1), Solar Plexus (2)
Subtle Body Affinities: Emotional/Mental, Etheric, Spiritual
Energy Focus: Building
Element: Water

Cocreating with Pink Tourmaline

Pink tourmaline is also helpful for a nonattached acceptance of things, and it has a more energetic, uplifting quality to it. You can work with it in a relationship when you wish to cut back on demanding that the other needs to change in order for you to be happy.

Pink Tourmaline Affirmation

"I ACCEPT YOU WITHOUT JUDGMENT AND WITHOUT EXPECTATIONS."

Watermelon Tourmaline—Physical Aspects

Watermelon tourmaline is a descriptive name given to a tourmaline that is red or pink inside and green outside. Polished cross sections are particularly striking.

The Watermelon Tourmaline Deva

From the moment that a lifestream incarnates into a physical vehicle, it comes into contact with other lifestreams who seek to pattern the new lifestream's energy according to their own beliefs and desires. I help you to learn the art of detachment through discernment, to identify who you are and who you are not in relationship to others. As you seek to change your point of reference in how you view yourself, my energy, through the power of Unconditional Love, helps you to release false identifications that do not reflect your true self. My synergistic blend of energies can unlock the door to greater self-acceptance and greater expansion on your spiritual path.

Watermelon Tourmaline—Spiritual Aspects

Soul Tone: D# when the piece has more pink, E when it has more green
Chakra Affinities: Lower Abdomen (1), Heart (1), Solar Plexus (2)
Subtle Body Affinities: Emotional/Mental, Etheric, Spiritual
Energy Focus: Building
Element: Water

Cocreating with Watermelon Tourmaline

Watermelon tourmaline blends the calm equanimity of green tourmaline with the more energetic upliftment of pink tourmaline. You could utilize it in situations where either pink or green tourmaline is appropriate.

Watermelon Tourmaline Affirmation

"I CALMLY RELEASE THE EXPECTATIONS OF OTHERS."

Black Tourmaline and
Black Tourmalinated Quartz—Physical Aspects

Black tourmaline is also called schorl. The black color is due in part to traces of iron. Although black tourmaline is very common, its energies seem to us quite "heavy," so we prefer to utilize black tourmalinated quartz, which is clear quartz with inclusions of black tourmaline.

The Black Tourmalinated Quartz Deva

My energies can give you a sense of protection and safety. Minerals do not just happen to bond their energy vibrations together by sheer chance. I can teach the Human Kingdom that light and darkness are not in mutual opposition. The clear quartz that is a part of my structure can amplify your sense of being surrounded and protected by the Light. The black tourmaline in my structure gives you a sense of safety. Each mineral works independently and yet we both work as one. The beauty and flexibility of my vibrations are such that you can program me to resonate to a particular color in your energy field to enhance the energy already present there.

Black Tourmalinated Quartz—Spiritual Aspects

Soul Tone: Black Tourmaline—C. Black Tourmalinated Quartz—all tones.

Chakra Affinities: Black Tourmaline—Root (1). Black Tourmalinated Quartz—all chakras.

Subtle Body Affinities: Emotional/Mental, Etheric, Spiritual

Energy Focus: Building

Element: Earth

Cocreating with Black Tourmalinated Quartz

The lightness and clarity of clear quartz amplifies the combination of emotional protection and balance of the black tourmaline. This energy is helpful for relationships in which you need to let go of expectations and need a sense of emotional protection and safety as well. Black tourmaline gives a quality of inner security, like being in a womb.

Black Tourmalinated Quartz Affirmation

"I AM EMOTIONALLY SAFE AND PROTECTED."

Blue Tourmaline—Physical Aspects

Blue tourmaline is also called indicolite. Its dark blue color is due to traces of iron.

Blue Tourmaline Deva

As do the other tourmalines, I teach you that both worrying about how things are happening, and desiring things to happen in a certain way, only slow down your expansion. In addition, I say to you to value truth as you understand it, no matter what others are doing. In doing so you may operate with or against the expectations of others. Remember that your purpose is to be in rhythm with the greater harmonies of the universe and to trust that by doing this you will have fulfilled your spiritual service. In this way you flow with focus.

Blue Tourmaline—Spiritual Aspects

Soul Tone: E

Chakra Affinities: Solar Plexus (1), Third Eye (1), Throat (2)

Subtle Body Affinities: Emotional/Mental, Spiritual, Etheric

Energy Focus: Building

Element: Water

Cocreating with Blue Tourmaline

Whenever you feel conflict between your Inner Spiritual Voice and the expectations of others, blue tourmaline can strengthen your understanding of the appropriate course of action. In this way you learn to value your own intuition and not to be swayed by the norms and values of society.

Blue Tourmaline Affirmation

"FOLLOWING THE BEAT OF MY OWN DRUMMER, I DO WHAT IS RIGHT FOR ME ON MY SPIRITUAL PATH, AND I RELEASE THE EXPECTATIONS OF OTHERS."

Turquoise

Physical Aspects

Turquoise, sometimes called callais, is an opaque stone that ranges from sky blue and blue-green to apple green. It is a hydrous phosphate of aluminum and copper, with a hardness of 5–6 and a triclinic crystalline structure. The pure blue color is rare, and traces of iron make it greener in color.

Turquoise is most commonly found in a matrix with veins of dark brown limonite, dark gray sandstone, black jasper, green malachite, and blue-green chrysocolla. The best quality occurs in nodules rather than veins, in northeastern Iran and Afghanistan. Turquoise is also mined the southwestern United States, Australia, and China.

Turquoise is very porous and is often impregnated with wax or plastic to deepen the color and add durability. There are several ways to tell whether turquoise has been impregnated. When turquoise has been plastic-bonded, you can carefully scrape it with a penknife and it will peel rather than powder, and give off an odor when heated. If it has been heavily waxed, a heated needle applied to the surface will melt the wax. Sometimes it is also dyed to deepen the color.

The Turquoise Deva

I teach you that Planet Earth and everything on it is a living, Spiritual Consciousness. I operate within your spiritual awareness rather than your conscious knowing. My energies help you to attune your vibrational energies to the spiritual essence within Nature's Mineral, Plant, and Animal Kingdoms.

I teach you about giving as well as receiving, not only from Planet Earth, but from your own Kingdom as well. If you of the Human Kingdom continue to hold the belief that you can "take" from Planet Earth and her Kingdoms without giving in return, you will not fully understand how the quality of your life has been reduced. I am a catalyst for initiating changes concerning your true relationship to the Earth. In this way you will heal the Earth Mother as well as yourselves.

Spiritual Aspects

Soul Tone: F#

Chakra Affinities: Heart (1), Thymus Gland (1)

Subtle Body Affinities: Spiritual, Etheric

Energy Focus: Spiritual Expansion

Element: Air/Earth

Cocreating with Turquoise

Turquoise strengthens the desire to be Earth stewards, and can be helpful when you wish to connect with the Mineral, Plant, or Animal Kingdoms. Turquoise strengthens your awareness of the interconnectedness of all life and is useful if you are feeling separate from others or from the natural world around you. Turquoise can also teach you to honor your physical body. Its gentle sense of interconnectedness has a healing effect and strengthens your awareness that we are all healers.

Affirmation

"I AM ONE WITH THE EARTH, AND I HONOR ALL LIFE WITH LOVE AND RESPECT."

Ulexite

Physical Aspects

Ulexite is popularly known as "the television stone." A piece of writing placed underneath the stone will appear enlarged on the surface of the stone. Some ulexites are translucent with a silky sheen, while others are a more opaque, satiny white. With a hardness of only 2 1/2, ulexite is a soft, fibrous stone. It is frequently found with other borate minerals and with calcite in the United States, Canada, Argentina, and Chile.

The Ulexite Deva

My purpose is one of vision, to help you understand your experiences with greater clarity. When you are feeling emotional pain or mental agitation, it can be difficult to perceive the meaning of an experience in your life. My energy helps you detach from worry, fear, and the concerns of your rational mind that can cloud your spiritual awareness. With greater understanding, you can go back into the experience without being weighted down by it, and act with greater freedom.

It is helpful to perceive your experiences not as problems, but as growth challenges. The challenge of becoming is learning to accept without judgment. When you doubt, my energies can show you what you will feel like or be like, once you have assimilated the truth of the experience itself. That vision becomes your ultimate motivation for action.

Spiritual Aspects

Soul Tone: A
Chakra Affinities: Third Eye
Subtle Body Affinities: Mental/Spiritual
Energy Focus: Clearing
Element: Air

Cocreating with Ulexite

Ulexite is a useful problem-solving or resolution stone because it detaches you from emotional imbalance and calms the mind when your thoughts seem agitated or stuck. You can place it on your third eye or hold it, and ask questions about the issue at hand. Ulexite is like a remote viewer in that it links a broader mental picture with greater spiritual understanding so that you can see the issues with greater clarity.

Ulexite has a sedative, relaxing effect when you need to take a mental break from too much intensity, or your energies are too scattered or agitated. Use it for stress reduction or meditation to help you calm and center your mind.

Affirmation

"I SEEK THE STILLNESS OF A GREATER CLARITY."

Vanadinite

Physical Aspects

The luster of vanadinite's small, red prismatic crystals make it an attractive stone in its rough form. Vanadinite is a soft stone, with a hardness of 3 and a hexagonal structure. It is a minor ore of lead that is often found with galena in the southwestern United States and in Mexico.

The Vanadinite Deva

There are times when you do not see the whole picture, and you must move into the void of the unknown. I tell you that you do not need to understand every aspect of your experience. Ask instead to be guided to those paths that will most enhance the quality of your life, and then continue on your journey with trust.

In order to move beyond feelings of insecurity about the unknown, it is important to build in your present moment a strong sense of self and confidence in your capacity to adapt to a new space.

A key quality in the growth process is timely action. When your vision is clouded, it may be because you are hesitating out of fear, or because you have acted impulsively. There is a difference between impulsivity and spontaneity. Spontaneous actions involve an infinite sense of creative exploration. Impulsive actions are often motivated by a need for the security of the known.

I can help you clarify the timeliness of your next steps, so that the process flows smoothly for you, and you are assured of a satisfactory completion. When you experience a lack of clarity in your vision, ask whether what you seek is indeed for your Highest Good. When your vision is clear and you are in harmony with your growth process, you will experience balance and peace.

Spiritual Aspects

Soul Tone: C#, D

Chakra Affinities: Solar Plexus, Root

Subtle Body Affinities: Mental/Spiritual

Energy Focus: Building

Element: Fire/Air

Cocreating with Vanadinite

Vanadinite encourages you to take a risk, in order to build upon that which is meaningful in your life. When you have firmly entrenched yourself in familiar ways of thinking about what you can accomplish, vanadinite gently guides your will in the direction that is in your best interests. Living in the void is like buying a plane ticket to an unknown destination. While you are on the plane, vanadinite helps you leave the familiar places behind, and accept the transit in space and time with more serenity. It can also help you assess the timeliness of your actions.

Affirmation

"I EMBRACE THE UNKNOWN WITH TRUST, VALUING EACH STEP IN MY PROCESS."

Yellow Orthoclase Feldspar (Yellow Sunstone)

Physical Aspects

Yellow orthoclase feldspar is a cloudy, yellow-green stone that is sometimes called yellow sunstone. However, it has a different chemical composition from orange sunstone, so we have taken the liberty of giving it a name that is descriptive of its mineral family. It is a potassium aluminum silicate member of the feldspar family with a hardness of 6–6 1/4. Gem-quality orthoclase is found in the Malagasy Republic and Upper Burma. There are also plentiful deposits in the United States

The Yellow Orthoclase Feldspar Deva

I help fine-tune your sense of timing in the activities of your life. Sometimes you choose to do things on emotional impulse, which can be unnecessarily risky. On other occasions you oversaturate yourself with information before you move on a decision. You may give more of your life-force energy to this process than you need to. I can help you find the middle road by heightening your perception of when it is time to make your decision and act on it. I give you a sense of reassurance that your decision is in a harmonious flow with the long-term goals you have for yourself. I can keep you from worrying about the "what ifs" so that you have a sense of flowing and being free for the expansion taking place in your life.

Spiritual Aspects

Soul Tone: E, D# (lighter stones test E. Darker and more opaque stones test D#)

Chakra Affinities: Solar Plexus (1), Lower Abdomen (2)

Subtle Body Affinities: Emotional/Mental, Etheric, Spiritual

Energy Focus: Building

Element: Water

Cocreating with Yellow Orthoclase Feldspar

If you are strongly attracted to yellow orthoclase feldspar at a particular time, you are probably being given a message that it is now time to make a move that you have been contemplating in some area of your life. It helps to keep you flowing so that you do not get bogged down in minor concerns and lose your focus. Yellow orthoclase feldspar thus helps with vacillation, indecision, and hesitancy through its warm, steady optimism and confidence.

Affirmation

"I MOVE FORWARD CONFIDENTLY ON MY PATH."

Zircon

Physical Aspects

The name zircon comes from the Persian zargun, which means "gold-colored." In nature, zircon is a gray-brown or red-brown prismatic stone of the tetragonal system, with a hardness of 6 1/2. However, zircons are often heat-treated to produce the colorless or gray zircons that are called jargoons, or red zircons that are called hyacinths. The purpose of heat-treating is to increase the brilliance and fire of zircon, and to produce yellow, orange, blue, and green zircons. The best gem-quality stones come from Ceylon, Burma, Cambodia, and France.

The Zircon Deva

One of the key areas of growth that challenges you of the Human Kingdom is the acceptance of change. I help to broaden your understanding of where you are in the moment and why movement into a new time and space is most encouraged. I work to help you prioritize your personal needs. You have the opportunity to honor those needs that are known to you, and to become more aware of those needs that have been covered in darkness. Once you see that you have choices that are positive and beneficial for you, then you can take that next step. Let your strengths be a foundation for your new space, and trust the rightness of moving forward.

Spiritual Aspects

Soul Tone: A

Chakra Affinities: Third Eye

Subtle Body Affinities: Emotional/Mental

Energy Focus: Building

Element: Air/Earth

Cocreating with Zircon

Zircon assists you in understanding the need for change. The guidance you receive may show you how you would develop more strength, clarity, or freedom as you move in your new direction. The guidance may also clarify the reasons that you need to shift, by pointing out needs that you are honoring.

Zircon can encourage you to let go of the past when you have been reluctant to change. It seems to assist you in continuing a change process that has already begun, rather than in instigating a new process. Zircon has a kind of empathic quality that says, "Pay attention to this important point, because this is the situation now from a broader perspective." Zircon is another of a number of stones that can ground and stabilize you in times of change. You can place it on any chakra where you are struggling with change, as well as on the third eye chakra.

Affirmation

"I ACCEPT THAT CHANGE IS HELPING ME HONOR MY NEEDS."

The Metals

Gold, silver, and copper are metallic elements that are included in this section to show how their energies combine in jewelry and other healing applications. Because the quality of their energy is more generalized or broadly focused than that of the minerals, they are more versatile in their use.

Copper

Physical Aspects

Copper is a metallic element (Cu) that can exist in a free, uncombined state. Besides the color of new pennies, copper can be black, blue, or green. It is a heavy, malleable mineral with a hardness of 2 1/2–3 and an isometric crystalline structure. Copper is mined in Michigan, Arizona, New Mexico, and Nova Scotia.

The Copper Deva

I seek to restimulate the flow of life-force energies where there has been constriction. My domain is the etheric subtle body and the physical vehicle itself. In order for me to be effective in your physical vehicle, you must be willing to change, for it is a restrictive way of thinking that causes an immobilization of life-force energy. Once the flow of life-force energy has been restored, other minerals such as clear quartz crystal can expand that flow. I can truly open your being so that you can relate to your Spiritual Nature in a more dynamic way.

Spiritual Aspects

Soul Tone: D

Chakra Affinities: Thymus Gland (1)

Subtle Body Affinities: Etheric, Spiritual

Energy Focus: Clearing

Element: Fire

Cocreating with Copper

Copper combines well in jewelry with stones that work in a clearing, dispersing capacity. It naturally occurs with malachite, azurite, and chrysocolla, and enhances their effect on the physical body. You can combine clear quartz crystal and copper by partially wrapping a crystal with copper wire, or making a wand with copper tubing and clear quartz crystal at the end. The copper will clear dense, imbalanced energy at the etheric subtle level, creating "space" for the amplification of life-force energies by the crystal. This combination gives a sense of movement and increased energy flow that is very effective for healing. A copper pyramid works in a similar manner.

Affirmation

"LIFE-FORCE ENERGY IS NOW FLOWING SMOOTHLY THROUGHOUT MY BODY, GIVING ME GREATER HEALTH AND VITALITY."

Gold

Physical Aspects

Gold is a metallic element (Au) that occurs in a free, uncombined state and rarely combines with other elements. It has a hardness of 2 1/2–3 and an isometric crystalline structure. Gold is heavier than pyrite and can yield a powder when hit with a hammer. It is currently mined in California, Colorado, Mexico, and Ontario.

The Gold Deva

My purpose is to enhance your connection with your Divine Nature so that you can reflect who you truly are. You can convert my energies to those qualities that enhance your self-identity and thereby affect your physical well-being. The quality of my energy is like the sun, and it has an activating effect on your energy system. The sun is a primary source of life-force energies. Like other stones, I radiate stored life-force energies that are originally from the sun throughout your being.

Spiritual Aspects

Soul Tone: E

Chakra Affinities: Root (1), Solar Plexus (1), Throat (1), Crown (1), Thymus Gland (1)

Subtle Body Affinities: Spiritual, Etheric

Energy Focus: Building

Element: Fire

Cocreating with Gold

Gold can amplify the life-force energy of stones with which it is combined. The amplification is strongest with stones that have a chakra affinity that is similar to the chakra affinities of gold. You can wear stones at the thymus gland with a gold chain and affirm your connection with your Divine Nature.

Affirmation

"I AM ACTUALIZING MY HIGHEST POTENTIAL."

Silver

Physical Aspects

Silver is a metallic element (Ag) that can be found in an uncombined state, although deposits sometimes include gold, mercury, copper, and other minerals. Besides its silvery color, it comes in whitish gray, yellow, brown, and black. Silver has a hardness of 2 1/2–3 and an isometric crystalline structure. It is widely distributed in small amounts, but the largest mines are in Michigan, Arizona, Colorado, Ontario, and Mexico.

The Silver Deva

I function primarily in the emotional subtle body as a gentle mover of energies that have become restricted or immobilized. My broadly focused energy can return you to emotional and mental stability. Because I am a single mineral I have more versatility in my function than a composite of minerals, which takes on a more specialized role. Work with me wherever you seek to grow, and I will help you begin the process of change.

Spiritual Aspects

Soul Tone: D

Chakra Affinities: Root (1), Lower Abdomen (1), Heart (1) Third Eye (1), Crown (2)

Subtle Body Affinities: Emotional, Spiritual

Energy Focus: Clearing

Element: Water

Cocreating with Silver

Silver settings can amplify stones with a similar chakra affinity. Silver jewelry can be worn at the heart to help you release constriction that keeps you from receiving and giving Unconditional Love. In general, silver can increase your sensitivity to your emotional nature. Its energies are gentle, harmonizing, and flowing.

Affirmation

"I AM IN HARMONY WITH MY EMOTIONAL BODY."

Part 3

COCREATING WITH
GEMSTONES FOR HEALING

N ow that you have been introduced to the individual stones, we can discuss ways to work with gemstones for healing yourself and others. Chapter 6 describes how to make and utilize gem essences for internal use. The use of essences has become more widespread since Edward Bach developed his flower remedies during the 1930s in England. In Chapter 7 we discuss some ways that you can utilize the stones for healing. The book concludes in Chapter 8 with some comments from the Devas on personal and planetary healing.

Changes on the planet are accelerating, both in your personal lives, and in the Kingdoms of Nature. Change is a natural part of the growth process, and you have a choice in how you respond to change. You can best co-create with Spirit by seeking to comprehend the messages that underlie your experiences. Responsible stewardship means that the Human Kingdom must bring itself into a greater alignment with the Kingdoms of Nature and with Mother Earth. Seek to be a clear channel of Light by acting according to the Highest Good, as you perceive it to be...

—Jonathan's Higher Self

Chapter 6

GEM ESSENCES: THEIR USE AND PREPARATION

When you are consciously working with attitudinal changes, gem essences can provide a balanced pattern of specific energy that operates like a subliminal tape, repeating positive messages over and over. However, also like a subliminal tape, it is sometimes hard to attribute changes directly to the essences. We have had experiences in which we noticed a dramatic release of discomfort in a given situation and other experiences in which it didn't seem like much happened. We are now able to sense the energy of the essences in our bodies, and have come to know more about how they work. Before that time we assumed on faith that they did work. You do not have to be aware of the essence in order for it to be effective. You just need to be willing to change.

This chapter includes some specific suggestions on making gem water and gem essences, and also how to go about choosing gem essences for yourself and others. At the end of the chapter, there are charts that you can use with a pendulum in order to determine the essences needed. For easy reference, we have also included a summary of the gemstone affirmations and soul tones at the end of the chapter.

Taking gem water internally is similar to taking herbs for healing purposes. However, taking herbs can more directly affect the etheric subtle body and the physical body. We are focusing more on affecting the emotional, mental, and spiritual subtle bodies with minerals, with the assumption that ultimately our overall health will be improved.

Water As a Medium for Energy Transfer

Water is very sensitive to energetic influence, and as in the case of clear quartz crystal, it has the capacity to store life-force energies. Science tells us that water is known as a good conductor of energy because its atoms have the tendency to both lose and gain electrons—it is an active medium for electron transfer.

Dr. Bernard Grad of McGill University conducted a number of experiments in the 1960s that demonstrate the physical effects of water that has been charged with life-force energy. He first had a healer hold the jar that contained salt water. A depressed psychiatric patient was asked to hold a second jar of salt water. A third jar was left untreated. Dr. Grad then soaked barley seeds in the three types of water and planted them. The barley seeds that had been soaked in the healer-treated water were taller and had greater chlorophyll content. The seedlings that had been soaked in water held by the depressed patient showed a suppressed growth rate.

A chemical analysis of the healer-treated water revealed changes in the atomic bonding angle, and decreased hydrogen bonding between the molecules. This decrease causes a corresponding decrease in the surface tension of the water. The experiment illustrates how water can be changed energetically without changing the water in any way.

The human body is composed of 40–80 percent water, depending upon the amount of fat, age, and gender. Water is the main constituent of body fluids. These body fluids include blood, lymph, cerebrospinal fluid, endolymph and philolymph of the ear, and the aqueous humours of the eye. Body water becomes a medium through which life-force energy can be transferred to all parts of the body.

According to the intuitive guidance of Kevin Ryerson, the energy of treated water initially enters through the bloodstream. The life-force energy is transferred to an electromagnetic network that exists between the circulatory system and the nervous system. From there it moves to the meridians, and then to the chakras, which transfer energy to the energy fields surrounding the body.

Life force energy vibrates at different frequencies. On a level that affects the physical body more directly it can be described as "vitality." At finer frequencies it can be described as "Consciousness." This is the level of energy that you utilize when you are calling on your Higher Self, or the Deva of the stone.

In the following sections we will describe two methods of programming water. We will call one method the "mechanical method" and it is the one developed by Dr. Bach in originating the Bach Flower Remedies. It utilizes the vitality of the sun to transfer the life-force energy of the flower (or the gemstone) to the water. It occurs without any conscious intervention other than putting a substance in a bowl of water and leaving it in the sunlight.

When you use a mechanical method to energize water, you must drink it right away, or you must add a preservative to the water. Without the constant stimulus of the sun, the water loses its particular charge over a period of time. Alcohol is the preservative commonly used in the current remedies and essences.

The second method we will call the "Consciousness method," where we merge in Oneness with both the water and the gemstone, and we change the structure of the water. With this method, the water does not lose its charge as quickly over a period of time, so you do not need to add a preservative. It is the same process as programming a crystal.

The Mechanical Method of Making Gem Essences

After you have cleaned and charged your gemstones, it is good to use them to make structured water. We will refer to the structured water that you drink on a daily basis as *gem water*. If you preserve the water and use it in eyedropper amounts, then we call it a *gem essence*. Gem essences have also been called gem remedies, gem elixirs, or gem tinctures.

Taking structured water internally is an excellent way to learn about the gemstones and to find out how the stones will work with your individual energies. The properties of the stones will give you some ideas about how the essences might work for you. It helps to keep records of how you are feeling when you take an essence, and the changes that occur. Then you will better know which stone you need in a given situation. You can develop your own rituals and methods for making gem waters and essences. Here are the steps we follow:

1. Place the stone in a clear glass container that has been sterilized by pouring boiling water into it. You can also place the glass container in an oven at 350 degrees for half an hour. If

you are making gem water, you might want to use a gallon container such as the glass jars that restaurants sometimes use for mayonnaise and pickles. If you are making an essence, you can use smaller glass jars or containers.

2.   Add spring or distilled water. In our experience, spring water is better. You can purchase either at the grocery store.

3.   Cover the container and place it outside in the sun. (We have also tried this process indoors under a pyramid and it does not work as well. Intuitively, we perceive that the Devas prefer to work outside of a pyramid.)

4.   Fill yourself with love and gratitude for the Elements of Nature and ask for Devic help in charging the water for healing.

5.   Leave the containers either for several hours, a day, or a day and a night, depending on the amount of water and your individual preferences. Gem water left out for 24 hours under the full moon carries the dynamic energies of both the sun and the moon. Moon energies are very beneficial for emotional healing.

Gem water used for drinking will last about three days at the most. If you wish to work with it on an ongoing basis, then you need to preserve it and it becomes a *gem essence.*

1.   You can buy 1-ounce brown eyedropper bottles at the drugstore either singly, or in boxes of one or two dozen.

2.   Sterilize them in boiling water for 15 minutes. Do not buy bottles with plastic eyedroppers because they bend when sterilized, and leave a taste in the essence. Also, they are not easy to resterilize.

3.   Fill the bottle halfway with your gem water.

4.   Fill the bottle the rest of the way with a good quality drinking alcohol such as brandy. (The alcohol is the only expensive part of this operation.) Now you have a gem essence that is 50 percent water and 50 percent alcohol.

5.   Label your bottles as "stock," such as "ruby stock," and store them under a pyramid or on a shelf out of the sunlight.

The Consciousness Method of Making Gem Essences

This method is a meditation, where you attune with the gemstone and project your sense of its energy into a jar of spring or filtered water. *The physical presence of the stone in the water is not necessary, because it is your focused spiritual intent that programs the water.* If you have one stone, you can hold it, attune with it, and project its essence into the water. If you have two stones of the same kind, you can merge with one stone, and place the other in the water (if you feel that having the stone in the water will strengthen your spiritual focus). A third choice is to meditate with one stone, clean it, and then place it in the water for the programming.

If you are working with a piece of jewelry containing several stones, focus your mind on the gemstone whose energy you wish to program into the water. An alternative is to program the composite energy of the jewelry into the water.

You can utilize a pendulum or other intuitive means of getting yes/no answers, in order to ask after each step whether you have completed it fully. Doing this will give you your own intuitive guidance about the programming process. Our experience has been that sometimes we are not fully balanced as we complete each step and it has to be done again. This happens because your thoughts can wander, you can be distracted, or you can worry so much about doing it right that you lower the quality of the energy that you are projecting. It took us some time to understand what some of the steps meant, which is a valuable learning process in itself. So be patient with yourself, especially the first time. You will find this meditation to be a powerful healing experience.

The following meditation is both channeled and created from our experience with the cocreative manifestation process. The steps are given in the form of an affirmation that you can use to begin each step. A brief explanation follows of the process involved with the affirmation. Once you get a sense of the process, you can omit the opening affirmation or develop your own. To work with this meditation you need to be in a comfortable space where you can work undisturbed:

Breathing deeply and slowly, inhale each color of the spectrum, pause, and exhale this color all through your body. Pause briefly and remain receptive. If the color seems a little muddy, breathe it again. You are realigning your system so that the essence that you create is more pure, and so that you can receive a greater understanding of the process.

"In order to bring myself into balance, I attune with the stone." Hold the stone in your hand, and sense how the energy of your body is being affected. Sense the message of the stone by asking for personal guidance, and trust whatever you receive, whether it is a symbol, an image, or a sense. You are attuning to what the stone means to you.

"I now choose what my focus is to be." Ask now for the highest energy expression of the stone. It may or may not be a little different from the personal message that you received. This is the energy sense that you are going to project into the water.

"I call in all aspects of Spirit who are needed in this process." Begin with calling in your Higher Self, and pause until your being is filled with this energy. Next call in the Deva of Water, and the Deva of the stone. Pause each time, and attune with the energy as best you can. You do not need to charge this water in the sun as you do in the mechanical method because you are charging the water with Consciousness. However, the sun's energy adds its own vitality to the water, so if you wish, you can also call in the Sun Deva.

"I ask for Devic help in opening the structure (or matrix) of the water." Place the jar of water in front of you and focus on it. You are asking permission of the water with honor and respect, because you are essentially changing its structure. Sense with humility the willingness of the Consciousness of the water to give service to you in this manner. You can visualize an area of Light opening in the water. Pause receptively until this process is completed.

"I ask that the Highest Spiritual Expression of this stone be permanently infused into the water." Focus with concentration on projecting the energy sense of the stone into the water. Try to discern when you have focused enough. For me, the thought energy seems to "bounce back" and it is less easy to focus intensely. Sometimes it feels like an electric current has shut off. Ask your pendulum if you have adequately focused the stone's energy into the water.

"I focus on what has been created and give thanks for it." Honor the creation of the energized water with gratitude, humility and joy. Breathe in the fullness of this experience, charging yourself with energy. Affirm your attunement with your Higher Will.

"I release my connection to the process, knowing it is now complete." Focusing on this statement helps you make a transition from being in a co-creative process with Spirit, to returning to everyday living.

You can place this essence in the sun for additional charging if you wish. It can be stored in a dropper bottle and taken as you would take an essence made by the mechanical method. One advantage of using this method is that it is easy to make larger quantities of water.

Taking the Gem Essences

Here are some guidelines for taking the essences:

1. It is best to determine intuitively how much to take. For example, you can start with two to five drops of an essence made by the mechanical method. You can also try small sips of water made by the consciousness method, at intervals.

2. Intuit how many times a day, for how many days. You can follow the general flower essence guidelines of taking the remedy four times per day for long-term personal growth. If you are upset and want to calm down, you can try two or three doses spaced at five-, 10-, or 15-minute intervals. We have found that taking a small number of drops at frequent intervals gives a more potent effect than taking a larger quantity of drops once or twice.

3. Shake the bottle vigorously for 15 seconds (count 1000...1 etc.) to activate the life force energy before taking it.

4. When you take the remedy, allow a quiet moment of receptivity and affirm that the Consciousness of the stone is helping you to heal. Work with your stone affirmations.

5. Allow at least a half-hour before or after eating before you take the remedy, so that the life force energy has a chance to affect your system. More time is even better.

6. Allow at least an hour before you take another energy medicine.

7. Keep your remedy covered, and do not touch the dropper to other surfaces or to the hands or inside the mouth. Store it out of direct sunlight.

8.   You can put the remedy directly on your skin, on meridian points, or in massage oil or topical cream.

9.   You can combine gem essences. You must use your intuition to do this because it is possible to create a dissonant energy flow with too many essences. We were most comfortable with single essences, and sometimes combined two or three. However, we had friends who combined more essences together and got effective results. It is a matter of belief and perception.

10. It is possible to become overcharged with a gem essence. Watch for any signs of dizziness or other symptoms of discomfort that arise when you take the essence. You have to discern these signals from uncomfortable issues that may surface as a result of taking the essences. This is a desirable effect, even though it may not seem so at the time.

11. Gem essences, unlike flower essences, can interfere with homeopathic remedies, so check with your homeopathic physician.

Figures 6-1 through 6-8 are charts that you can use with a pendulum to determine which essence to take and what dosage. The stones are organized according to our perceptions of the chakra affinities. We have also included a list of the stone affirmations.

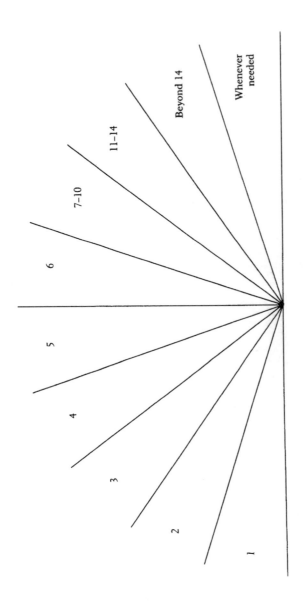

Figure 6-1. How often & how much essence

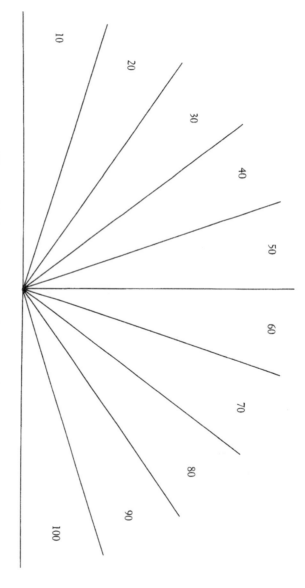

Figure 6-2. Percentage correlation for essences

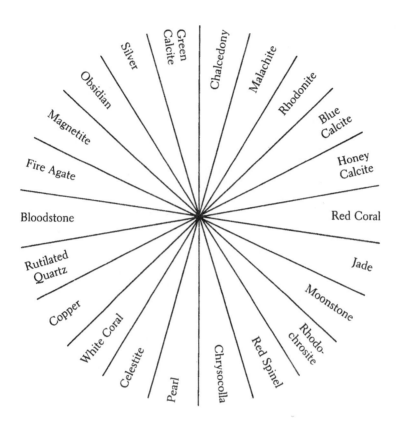

Figure 6-3. Clearing:
Gemstones and essences—Root through throat chakras

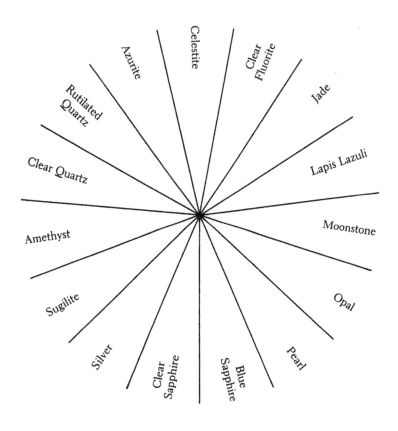

Figure 6-4. Clearing:
Gemstones and essences—Third eye and crown chakras

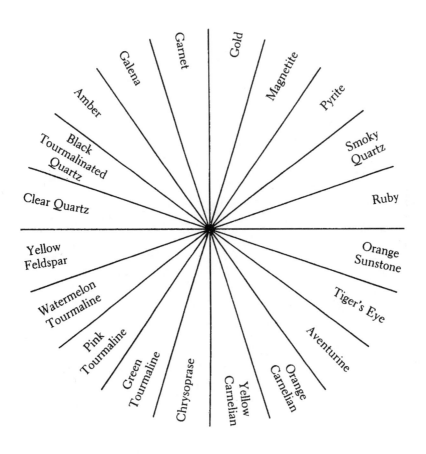

Figure 6-5. Building and spiritual expansion:
Gemstones and essences—Root and lower abdomen chakras

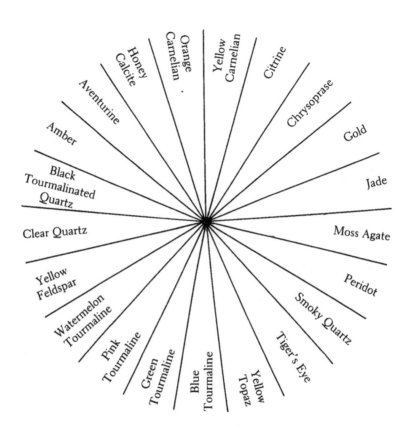

Figure 6-6. Building and spiritual expansion:
Gemstones and essences—Solar plexus chakras

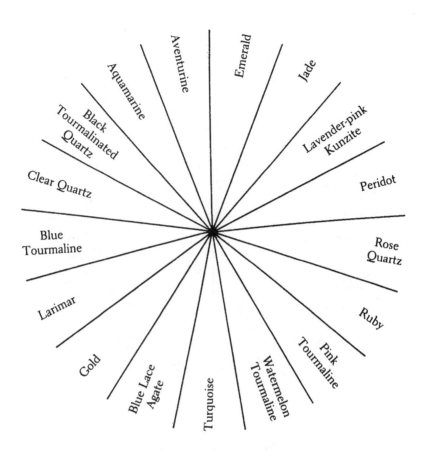

Figure 6-7. Building and spiritual expansion:
Gemstones and essences—Heart and throat chakras

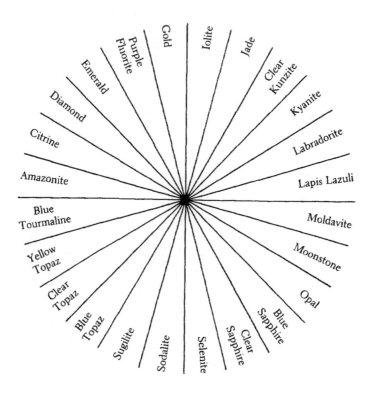

*Figure 6-8. Building and spiritual expansion:
Gemstones and essences—Third eye and crown chakras*

Gem Essence for Clients

We use gem essences with clients at the beginning of a healing session, and sometimes as a session in itself when the client wishes to use the essences on an ongoing basis. Here are the steps we follow:

1. Before beginning the process take an essence that balances you and helps you to release your personal will.

2. Hold the client's sending hand in your receiving hand, and hold the pendulum in your sending hand. Both of you should breathe deeply, relax, and center. Affirm that you are finding the essence that is for the highest good of the client at this time. The client can affirm openness to Higher Guidance.

3. Choose an essence with the client (see Figure 6-3 through Figure 6-8).

   a. Use a chart in the form of a circle or an arc and ask the pendulum to "Point to the essence that the client needs for his/her highest good at this time." Hold the pendulum over the center point of the circle, or the midpoint of the baseline of the arc.

   b. You can put your bottles in groups and ask, "Is there an essence in this group that the client needs for his/her highest good at this time?"

   c. Honor your intuitive insights about what the client needs, or what the client feels he or she needs.

4. Double-check your choice by placing the essence bottle in the client's receiving hand and asking the pendulum, "Is this the essence needed at this time?" Note the strength of the yes (see Figure 6-2).

5. It is possible to combine gem essences. Ask your pendulum, "Point to another essence needed at this time on this chart," or "Is there any other essence needed at this time?" Have the client hold the combination(s) of essences and ask, "Is this the most appropriate combination of essences at this time?"

6. Once you have determined the essence(s), you can determine the timing and the number of drops (see Figure 6-1). With your pendulum ask the following questions:

a. "Is the essence to be taken now, for one time only?"

b. If the answer is no, use an arc and ask the pendulum to show you the number of days the essence is to be taken.

c. If you or the client are to take the essence whenever needed, we have found it effective to take the essence when the need arises, and then every 10 or 15 minutes until a sense of balance returns. Usually two or three times is sufficient.

d. Use the same arc and ask to be shown the number of drops to be taken at one time.

e. If more than one essence is to be taken sequentially, allow a minimum of 15 minutes between essences.

7. Share with the client the purpose of the essence and the appropriate affirmations. Encourage a conscious focusing on the spiritual qualities of the stone whenever the essence is taken (see Figure 6-9).

8. After the client takes the essence, you can both sound the soul tone of the stone to amplify its effect, and sit quietly for a bit.

The effect of the gem essences can be minimized when you are consuming substances that alter the body's metabolism, such as coffee, alcohol, and cigarettes. For example, try not to follow the gem essence with a cup of coffee or a cigarette. Instead, take the gem essence and work with the affirmations as a special "mini-break" time of self-nurturing. Also, gem essences (unlike flower essences) can interfere with homeopathic remedies, so check with your homeopathic physician.

Figures 6-3 through 6-8 are charts for choosing gem essences with a pendulum. The stones are organized according to the chakra affinities in order to aid in choosing a stone to place on a particular chakra for healing work.

Figure 6-9.
Gemstone Affirmations and Soul Tones

Alexanderite
A#
"I open to the greater possibilities that change is bringing to my spiritual growth."

Amazonite
A, A#
"I am protected by the Light as I move through transitions in my life, and I bless what I have accomplished."

Amber
C
"I build my physical vitality through lightness of spirit."

Amethyst
B
"I release all need for self-identity."

Apatite
E
"I act with foresight, in harmony with All That Is."

Aquamarine
G
"I am reassured and uplifted by the knowledge that my work is my love made visible."

Aventurine
E
"I expand my vision of who I can be."

Azurite
G#, G
"I find peace as I release emotional ties from the past."

Bloodstone
C#, C
"I affirm the power of my perseverance to see me through all situations."

Blue Lace
Agate
G#
"I reflect calm inner certainty, as I speak with non-judgment and discernment."

Green Calcite
D
"I release nervous tension and feel calm and relaxed."

Blue Calcite
E

"I affirm safety and peace during times of intensity."

Honey Calcite
D#

"I remain optimistic during times of intensity."

Orange
Carnelian
D

"I find something positive to enjoy in every aspect of my life."

Yellow
Carnelian
D#

"I enjoy the gifts of my everyday life with all my senses."

Celestite
G

"My mind is relaxed and open to connect with my Higher Guidance."

Chalcedony
D to E

"I trust the messages my feelings are giving me and I speak up for what I need."

Charoite
A#

"I forgive myself, and I am forgiven and accepted by Spirit."

Chrysocolla
F, F#, or G

"I listen to my heart to find and affirm my spiritual purpose."

Chrysoprase
D

"Completing one step at a time connects me with my inner roots and gives me a sense of continuity in my life."

Citrine
E

"I think and communicate clearly, synthesizing information from all levels of my being."

White Coral
G, G#

"I listen to that which is for my Highest Good and I release all else."

Red Coral
E

"I honor both my own unique path and the unique paths of others, by taking decisive action without judgment."

Diamond
B

"The purity of my actions reflects the moral code by which I live my life."

Dioptase F	"I dissolve the voice of my inner judge with Unconditional Love."
Emerald F	"I joyfully give thanks for the abundance in my life."
Fire Agate D	"I move forward with focus and direction and affirm that every moment is a new beginning."
Clear Fluorite A#, A	"I release my personal will in order to purify my awareness."
Purple Fluorite A, B	"As I merge with Divine Will, I find greater peace and illumination."
Galena All tones	"I integrate my spiritual awareness by establishing my priorities and acting upon them."
Garnet C	"I affirm my reservoir of inner strength and I act with practicality."
Gem Silica A#	"I affirm my spiritual purpose in the world with joy and trust."
Heliodor A#	"I reach for the Light of Greater Wisdom to assist me in changing my beliefs."
Hematite F	"As I release emotional pain, I am freed to take action."
Iolite B	"I open to greater personal and spiritual growth through communication with my soul."
Jade E	"My body, mind, and spirit are in perfect balance."
Jasper C#	"I creatively express the joy of being alive, in everything that I do."
Jet C#	"I accept both the reality of change, and my eternal Oneness with Spirit."
Lavender-pink Kunzite F	"I live my life zestfully and creatively to the fullest."

Clear Kunzite A	"I create to my highest capacity my vision of Light."
Kyanite A#	"My physical body is a sacred temple built of pure Love."
Labradorite B	"I now access the Akashic Records in order to expand my spiritual growth."
Lapis Lazuli G#, A	"I seek the truth in understanding my experiences."
Larimar G	"I fulfill my spiritual service in a way that is uniquely my own, to help others understand the unlimited nature of growth and knowledge."
Lepidolite D#–E	"I shift my focus from stimulation to balance, in order to enjoy my life more fully."
Magnetite C#	"I trust my abilities to accelerate change."
Malachite E, F	"I have the courage and determination to work through all fear."
Moonstone G#, A	"I value my emotional sensitivity, knowing that it is all right to feel what I am feeling."
Moldavite B	"I go beyond limited thinking and receive the Unconditional Love present in other dimensions of the universe."
Moss Agate E	"I initiate action to understand the spiritual dimension in all physical reality."
Obsidian C, C#	"Letting go of my resistance to looking inward frees my personal power to bring about change."
Opal A	"I am now free, independent, and creative, as I expand beyond perceived limitations from my past."
Pearl A	"As I risk myself emotionally in order to heal, I am protected and nurtured."

Peridot
E
"Inner joy lights my way, and I share that joy with others."

Pyrite
C
"I open to receive additional life-force energy wherever it is needed."

Rhodochrosite
F
"I accept that I am truly a lovable being, and I forgive those who have forgotten that they are loved."

Rhodonite
D#
"I release my longing for the past as I find in every day something beautiful and new for me to appreciate."

Rose Quartz
F
"I delight in play and pleasure."

Ruby
F#, F
"I have the courage and strength to be who I truly am."

Rutilated Quartz
All tones
"I can now see clearly beyond the illusions of my past."

Clear Sapphire
A#
"I have faith and trust in the process of my growth toward the Light."

Blue Sapphire
A
"Knowing that I am actively guided and supported in my growth toward the Light brings me peace."

Selenite
A#, A
"I affirm my connection with my Spirit Guides."

Smoky Quartz
C
"I find security in knowing that I can learn, whether I win or lose."

Sodalite
A, A#
"My mind is calm and ordered so that I can concentrate with a singular focus."

Red Spinel
E
"I strengthen my sense of self and my inner fulfillment as I complete my tasks in life."

Sugilite
A#
"I am a Divine Manifestation of Love."

Orange Sunstone D#	"There is no limit to what I can do."
Tiger's Eye C#	"My belief in my purpose and my strength is the active foundation for my personal power."
Clear Topaz A#	"I joyfully expand the horizons of my spiritual understanding."
Yellow Topaz E	"I seek to comprehend the practical wisdom in all my experiences, and I manifest that wisdom."
Blue Topaz A	"I calmly accept the implications of my expanding spiritual understanding."
Black Tourmaline C	"I am emotionally safe and protected."
Black Tourmalinated Quartz All tones	"I am emotionally safe and protected."
Blue Tourmaline E	"Following the beat of my own drummer, I do what is right for me on my spiritual path, and I release the expectations of others."
Green Tourmaline E	"I let go of my inner expectations about how my life needs to be."
Pink Tourmaline D	"I accept you without judgment and without expectation."
Watermelon Tourmaline D#, E	"I calmly release my expectations of others."

Turquoise F#	"I am One with the Earth and I honor all life with love and respect."
Ulexite A	"I seek the stillness of a greater clarity."
Vanadinite C#–D	"I embrace the unknown with trust, valuing each step in my process."
Yellow Orthoclase Feldspar E, D#	"I move forward confidently on my path."
Zircon A	"I accept that change is helping me to honor my needs."

Metals

Copper D	"Life-force energy is now flowing smoothly throughout my body, giving me greater health and vitality."
Gold E	"I am actualizing my highest potential."
Silver D	"I am in harmony with my emotional body."

Chapter 7

GEMSTONES AND HEALING

Now that you have been introduced to the individual stones, we offer some suggestions for utilizing the stones for personal healing. To share in a healing process with the stones, or with other people, is to experience the awe, joy, and compassion of spiritual communion. The manner in which you experience the healing process, as well as how you utilize the stones in this work, determines how they affect you. In healing work you are "programming" or "focusing" the energy of stones in a particular manner for a particular purpose.

A good healing meditation is to hold a stone or take its essence, and ask the Higher Consciousness of the stone to assist you in healing. Then breathe deeply and hold the focus of your Oneness with the stone. Be aware of the energy sensations in your body, because the stone will stimulate the movement of blocked energy.

Another way you can work is to focus your intent on the affirmations for the individual stones and ask that the stones add their energy to your particular affirmations.

Alternatively, you can place a stone on your Third Eye chakra and direct its energies wherever needed. Hypoallergenic tape can secure the stone to your forehead so that you can either sit up or lie down.

The Thymus Gland

The thymus gland and the heart chakra seem to have separate locations on the body and separate but interrelated functions. The heart chakra is generally shown as being located in the center of the chest, between the breasts. You can find the thymus gland about halfway between heart and throat chakra, and it is generally a sensitive area.

The thymus gland receives spiritual life-force energies that come from our awareness and acceptance of the spiritual dimension in life, and transforms them for use in the physical body. The thymus gland is an indicator of the overall life-force vitality, or the level of physical balance in the body. In other words, physical health is related to our openness to receive Unconditional Love.

The heart chakra *receives* life-force energy and *transforms* it for use on the emotional and mental levels, and it is also where we *give* compassion to others. Therefore, the heart chakra is one indicator of emotional and mental well-being.

We believe that it is useful to work with stones on both the heart chakra and the thymus gland, in order to open all levels of the being to the vitality of Unconditional Love. When you seek to understand the level of physical balance in the body, the thymus gland can be an initial contact point. There are several ways that you can do this:

1. Use a muscle-testing procedure to test the strength of the thymus gland. This requires two people:

    ♦ The client holds the left arm straight out to the side, parallel to the floor. The client then places the fingertips of the right hand midway between the throat and the line of the breasts, in the middle of the chest. This is the area of the thymus gland.

    ♦ Facing the client, the tester places the left hand on the client's shoulder and the right hand on the client's extended arm, above the wrist.

    ♦ On the count of three the client pushes his arm up and the tester presses down. If the thymus gland is strong, the arm shouldn't move. If it's weak, you will push the arm down easily. (If you repeat this test and ask the client to think of negative and then positive thoughts, you will notice that the thymus gland tests stronger with the positive thoughts.)

- If there is a lack of physical vitality due to a long-standing imbalanced belief, the area may test weak.

2. Hold a pendulum over the thymus gland and ask the pendulum to indicate the strength of the gland.

3. Scan the thymus gland area with your hand, and sense for any restrictions of life force energy.

Here are some ways that you can activate the thymus gland and strengthen the immune system, by opening yourself to life-force energy in various forms:

1. Seek assistance in discovering the underlying subconscious beliefs that may be affecting your health. Appreciate and affirm health in your physical body.

2. Receive the Unconditional Love that pours into you from Nature and from other beings.

3. Discover and affirm the spiritual purpose of your life.

4. Wearing stones at the thymus gland can help. Affirm the qualities of the jewelry when you put it one, and ask that your receive its energies throughout the day.

5. Place a stone on the thymus gland during healing sessions.

6. Activate the gland with sound.

7. When you are in the sunlight, consciously affirm that you are taking in the life-force energy of the sun for the health and well-being of your physical body.

8. Stimulate the area by tapping it lightly with your fingers up to about 25 times. Then sense the energy of the thymus gland.

It is possible to overstimulate the thymus gland by giving it too much attention too quickly. Some signs of overstimulation are jitteriness and feeling "hyped up." You can release an overcharge by mentally visualizing the energy at the thymus gland dispersing to all parts of your body.

Here is a listing of stones and metals that we have found to have an affinity for the thymus gland:

Turquoise	Amethyst
Moss agate	Clear quartz crystal
Moldavite	Rutilated quartz
Amazonite	Gold

3 Criteria for Layouts

By laying more than one stone on the body you can create more complex energy patterns that affect larger areas of the body. However, the compatibility of the stones becomes very important. The aim is to create a heightened and unified energy field rather than a diffusion of diverse frequencies. An important factor in combining stones is *how you personally attune with them in creating an energy field.*

In our work we have chosen to focus on the chakra system. By placing a stone on each chakra, we create an "energy circuit" that affects all of the subtle bodies. It appears that by connecting the chakras, the energy created is greater than the sum of its parts. Small stones used in a pattern on a particular chakra have greater potency than when utilized singly, because of the current of energy that is created. We developed three criteria for layouts.

The first criterion is the stones' affinity for a particular chakra. Stones that have an affinity for a specific chakra affect all of the subtle bodies more strongly. We experimented with layouts using compatible stones but we placed them on chakras for which they did not have a primary affinity. We discovered that they effectively balanced the spiritual subtle bodies, but not necessarily the emotional and mental subtle bodies.

The second criterion is compatibility of frequency. Stones with compatible frequencies are well attuned in the manner that they move energy, as well as the density of energy with which they work. This can create a unified flow that is very smooth. For example, we state earlier that "clearing" stones that disperse denser energy are more likely to be compatible. Relating stones to the Elements of Earth, Air, Fire, and Water, *as you perceive them* is an effective way to combine stones.

Stones that are not well-attuned can sometimes create uncomfortable sensations. A sign of incompatibility among stones on the body can be a feeling of pressure or tingling on the hands, or erratic energy movements in the body.

In layouts where there is a compatibility of frequency at the spiritual subtle body level but not at the other levels, one particular stone may serve as a unifying energy. The layout will not flow without that stone. In more highly compatible layouts, a stone can be removed and the layout will still flow.

The third criterion relates to a compatibility of purpose. For example, if you are building self-empowerment, you will choose stones that speak to you of confidence and courage. Affirm your mental focus and ask your Higher Self to guide you to the appropriate stones.

We also experimented with groupings of minerals such as the tourmaline family and found that they work well together. Another combination like this includes the copper related minerals of malachite, chrysocolla, and azurite.

Working With 1 or 2 Stones

When you work with one or two stones on the body at a time, you have more choices about where to place the stones for healing. In all examples, we ask the Mineral Deva or Higher Guidance to work with us, focusing the energy to the areas in need:

1. For self-healing, you can place a stone on the third eye and direct its energies wherever needed. You can use hypoallergenic tape to secure the stone on the third eye so that you can either sit up or lie down. The third eye is able to interpret different kinds of input and then direct energy according to that input.

2. For self-healing, hold a stone or take its essence and focus your intention on locating where in your body you are holding imbalanced energy. The stone acts as a radar device that locates and amplifies restricted energy where clearing needs to take place. Kyanite and sugilite, as well as other stones to which you may be attracted, can aid you in this process.

3. When working with others, scan the body with your sensing hand to locate imbalances, and intuitively decide where your energy work will have the greatest impact. Often this will be the area that is most out of balance. Hold the stone in your sending hand about a foot above the body and direct energy into the affected area.

4.   You can also hold the stone in your sending hand above the body, and make clockwise circles until you have the sense that the area has received what it needs. This is the infusing position described in Chapter 4.

Figure 7-1. Clockwise Infusion.

Choosing and Working With a Layout

We often begin by choosing a stone intuitively for the Third Eye. You can ask what stone would be best, and wait receptively for the answer, or you can dowse with a pendulum. The charts at the end of Chapter 6 can be helpful for this purpose. Next, choose a stone for the heart, solar plexus, or the most imbalanced chakra. The third eye stone and the stones for imbalanced chakras will determine the nature of the layout. The other choices in the layout can be made according to the qualities of the stones involved, or what feels appropriate on a given chakra.

Depending on your own skills and training, there are two methods of working with a layout. One way is to place a layout on your body to balance the energy field, and then work with other therapeutic skills. For example, if you would like to do a past-life regression, you can create a layout that helps disperse blocked energy while you focus on the past-life process.

The other method is to focus your energy primarily on the stones. Begin at the root chakra, and ask the Consciousness of the stone to be present with you. Then visualize your root chakra being filled with Light. Continue to hold this focus until you sense that the root chakra has received all the energy that it can integrate at this time. Repeat this process with the other chakras.

We have included two charts of chakra affinities that you may find helpful as a starting point for creating your own layouts. Keep in mind however that these are our perceptions and it is important to place your gemstones wherever your Inner Knowing guides you to place them.

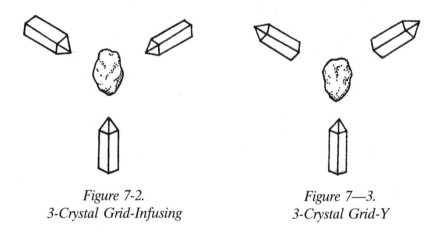

Figure 7-2.
3-Crystal Grid-Infusing

Figure 7—3.
3-Crystal Grid-Y

Gemstones and Clear Quartz Crystal

The amplifying properties of clear quartz crystal make it a powerful addition to any layout. Here are some suggestions for combining gemstones and clear quartz crystals:

1. Place clear quartz crystal at the Crown Chakra. This can strengthen your connection with Spirit in any layout.

2. Glue or place a tiny stone onto a clear quartz crystal to amplify its energies.

3. Place a drop of the gem essence onto the termination of a clear quartz crystal and point it toward the stone on the body.

4. Utilize a treated crystal in place of a stone. The advantages are that you can choose to buy an essence for an expensive stone such as the diamond rather than the diamond itself, and thus experience a wider variety of stone energies. We also found that sometimes others were more comfortable with a treated crystal on the third eye chakra, than they were with the stone on the third eye. The disadvantage is that the energy seems a little weaker than that of the stone itself. Utilizing crystals with essences can give you more flexibility in your healing work.

5. Crystals work well when placed in a *grid,* which is a geometric pattern of stones that creates a vortex of energy. We especially like to use a Star of David grid of six crystals at the Crown Chakra in a layout. You can also place a stone in a clear crystal grid of three, four, five, or six stones on any chakra, and treat the crystals' terminations with the stone's essence (see Figures 7-2 and 7-3). If you utilize the crystals without treating them, you get more "clear crystal energy" and less "stone energy," which is a viable option.

ROOT	LOWER ABDOMEN	SOLAR PLEXUS	HEART	THYMUS	THROAT	THIRD EYE	CROWN
Bloodstone C#, C	Bloodstone C#, C	Blue Calcite E	Jade E	Clear quartz	Celestite G	Amethyst B	Clear Quartz
Fire Agate D	Green Calcite D	Honey Calcite D#	Malachite E, F	Amethyst B	Chrysocolla G, F#	Azurite G#, G	Amethyst B
Clear Fluorite A#, A	Chalcedony E, D	Chalcedony E, D	Rhodochrosite F	Moldavite B	White Coral G, G#	Celestite G	Clear Fluorite A#, B
Hematite F	Fire Agate D	Red Coral E	Silver D	Rutilated Quartz		Charoite A#	
Magnetite C#	Hematite F	Hematite F				Clear Fluorite A#, A	
Obsidian C#, C	Obsidian C#, C	Jade E				Heliodor A#	
Silver D	Rhodonite D#	Malachite E, F				Jade E	
	Silver D	Moonstone G#, A				Lapis Lazuli G#, A	
		Rhodonite D#				Moonstone G#	
		Red Spinel E				Opal A	
						Pearl A	
						Blue Sapphire A	
						Clear Sapphire A#	
						Sugilite A#	
						Ulexite A	

All Chakra Affinities: Clear Quartz, Rutilated Quartz.
No Chakra affinities: Copper.

Figure 7-4.
Gemstone Chakra Affinities for Clearing

Figure 7-5.
Gemstone Chakra Affinities for Building and Spiritual Expansion

ROOT	LOWER ABDOMEN	SOLAR PLEXUS	HEART	THYMUS	THROAT	THIRD EYE	CROWN
Amber C	Amber C	Amber C	Dioptase F	Clear Quartz	Aquamarine G	Alexandrite A#	Clear Quartz
Garnet C	Aventurine E	Apatite E	Emerald F	Amazonite A	Blue Lace Agate-G#	Amazonite A	Alexandrite A#
Gold E	Orange Carnelian D	Aventurine E	Jade E	Copper D	Chrysocolla G, F, F#	Citrine E	Diamond B
Jasper C#	Chrysoprase D	Honey Calcite D#	Lavender-pink Kunzite-F	Gold D#	Gold D#	Diamond B	Iolite B
Jet C#	Hematite F	Orange Carnelian D	Peridot E	Moldavite F	Larimar G	Purple Fluorite A, B	Labradorite B
Magnetite G#	Lepidolite D#, E	Yellow Carnelian D#	Rose Quartz F	Moss Agate E		Gem Silica A#	Moldavite B
Pyrite C	Orange Sunstone D#	Chrysoprase D	Ruby F#	Turquoise F#		Iolite B	
Smoky Quartz C	Tiger's Eye C#	Citrine E	Pink Tourmaline-D			Jade B	
Ruby F#	Green Tourmaline-E	Dioptase F	Watermelon Tourmaline-E			Clear Kunzite E	
Orange Sunstone-D#	Pink Tourmaline-D	Gold E	Turquoise F#			Kyanite A	
Tiger's Eye C#	Watermelon Tourmaline-D#	Jade E				Labradorite A#	
Black Tourmaline-C	Yellow Feldspar-E, D#	Lepidolite D#, E				Lapis Lazuli G#	
Vanadinite C#, D		Moss Agate E				Moldavite B	

Figure 7-5. (Continued)
Gemstone Chakra Affinities for Building and Spiritual Expansion

ROOT	LOWER ABDOMEN	SOLAR PLEXUS	HEART	THYMUS	THROAT	THIRD EYE	CROWN
		Peridot				Moonstone	
		E				G#, A	
		Tiger's Eye				Opal	
		C#				A	
		Yellow Topaz				Blue Sapphire	
		E				A	
		Blue				Clear Sapphire	
		Tourmaline-E				A#	
		Green				Selenite	
		Tourmaline-E				A#, A	
		Vanadinite				Sodalite	
		C#, D				A, A#	
		Yellow Feldspar				Sugilite	
		E, D#				A#	
						Blue Topaz	
						A	
						Yellow Topaz	
						E	
						Blue	
						Tourmaline-E	
						Zircon	
						A	

All Chakra Affinities: Clear quartz, Black Tourmalinated Quartz.
No Chakra Affinities: Galena.

Conclusion

Creating layouts is a powerful way to utilize the stones. Our clients have had dramatic results with the release of memories, past-life traumas, and other energy blocks, through the use of layouts. We have restored our inner balance and sense of peace, and strengthened our spiritual priorities. Attuning with the stones has assisted us in affirming who we are, and moving toward new possibilities in our personal growth.

It is important to say here that attuning with the Consciousness of gemstones is only one approach to healing. We have wrestled with the question of whether or not we could help others effectively without the gemstones or other healing tools that we have explored. One conclusion is that our desire to explore gemstones was guided by Spirit so that we could develop a more profound relationship to the world of physical form. When you know that everything is alive you honor the environment in new ways, and you expand your perspective on the changes that are happening on the Earth.

The other conclusion is that our own sensitivity to life-force energy and our ability to work with it has increased. It is not the quantity or power of the tools that is important. It is the depth of your own spiritual attunement that strengthens your capacity to channel healing energy. And so we say, enjoy your explorations and anticipate the changes that you will bring about in your own life with joy, wisdom, and peace.

Chapter 8

PLANETARY OVERVIEW

W e conclude with the messages from the Overlighting Deva of the Mineral Kingdom and the Overlighting Deva for Planet Earth.

The Overlighting Deva of the Mineral Kingdom

The evolutionary cycle of all beings on the Planet is ordered to emphasize the interdependence among all species, both in physical and spiritual development. The spiritual evolutionary cycle can be described as follows: Consciousness manifests in the world of form, in direct connection with the Divine Source. The ability to create with form then evolves, along with the increasing responsibility for the forms created. Finally, Consciousness creates a state of formlessness, totally connected to the Divine Source. A mutually supportive way of being is a necessary condition for all life forms to evolve into their highest level of being. To us, no Kingdom is ever perceived as greater in its inherent capacities than any other.

The central focus for spiritual evolution in all Kingdoms, including the Human Kingdom, is to serve Planet Earth from a space of Pure Unconditional Love and Light. You of the Human

Kingdom have the capacity to create through the use of your mind and will. When these gifts are exercised with due regard for all other life forms, Planet Earth exists in a state of balance and can receive increased spiritual energies. There is abundance present everywhere. When the mind and will of the Human Kingdom are directed toward the satisfying of personal desires rather than consideration of the collective effect on Nature of such actions, this creates imbalanced energies that affect the evolvement of all forms of life.

The Mineral Kingdom gives service to all of life by providing a stable balance for the planetary structure. The Mineral Kingdom receives its life-force energies from the sun and from other sources beyond the planet. All other Kingdoms depend on the form and balance given by the life-force energies of the Mineral Kingdom. You must have a foundation to have life.

The minerals bring to the Human Kingdom spiritual qualities that can be expressed in human form. Your very physical structure is made up of minerals and therefore can manifest the spiritual qualities of those minerals. Personality and will originate from the minerals and plants that are a part of the physical body. As your awareness changes you can change the vibrational effects which the minerals, as a part of your body, have on your total being. Now you know how deeply you create your reality.

The Mineral Kingdom evolves through the complexity of form and through the graduating levels of higher spiritual energies. Minerals learn that they can give and receive life-force energies without leaving the space they occupy. This is a lesson of form. There is a transference of energy that takes place as part of the evolutionary process. This may manifest as a new physical structure, or a nonphysical increase in the life-force energy. Just as more human lifestreams are becoming more aware of the time of transition from the present physical reality, so the Spiritual Consciousness of the mineral knows when the time has come to evolve to another level of beingness. It is all a learning process which each life form enacts time and again, toward greater perfection and refinement of the energies of Self.

Just as the Human Kingdom is capable of receiving from the Mineral Kingdom that which is needed to balance individual energy systems, so too must lifestreams reciprocate in their interrelationship with the other Kingdoms of Nature. Whenever the Human Kingdom displaces any mineral from its origin, a void is created that must be filled either by Nature herself or by the Human Kingdom. 'Balance can be restored, for example, by replacing the minerals taken with new plant life.

An "energy light grid" that is the etheric subtle body of the planet surrounds Planet Earth. This light grid provides the exterior framework through which Planet Earth's form is maintained. Contained within this outer grid are internal light grids that are formed through interlocking that takes place among mineral, plant, and animal species at their locations throughout the planet. The more widely distributed a species is, the greater the internal grid pattern it weaves as part of the planet's structure.

Fractures or upheavals within the earth's body, caused by human or natural sources, disconnect the internal light grids. If allowed to continue in this state, imbalance will exist not only in that area, but throughout the planet, since all energy is interconnected. When you hold in your mind the focus of harmony and flow of life-force energies in any imbalanced area, you are helping to bring healing energies and balance the Planet Earth.

To do this, picture Planet Earth in your third eye with spokes of pure White Light emanating from her North and South pole areas, and enveloping the planet in a large ball. When you hold this vision in a meditative state with clear quartz crystal, you amplify the external light grid that maintains earth's form. See the energy as a moving rainbow of colors, infusing the earth with the gifts of each ray. The choices that you make in how you give your energy can reflect the same quality of pure Unconditional Love that is given to you by the Kingdoms of Nature.

The Overlighting Deva for Planet Earth

Hear my words, beloved lifestreams of my Human King-dom. I do not condemn or pass any judgment on the actions that you have taken as you continue your stay on my physical body. I am your Mother even as you have mothers in the flesh. My Un-conditional Love for each lifestream in the Human Kingdom re-mains eternally present with you. In times past you were more consciously aware of my needs and therefore took appropriate action to see that they were met. This was possible because you had felt deep inside your being an Unconditional Love for self that in turn guided you into a right relationship with all life forms, including myself.

Over a period of time, the overall focus for the Human King-dom has dramatically changed. You judge yourselves and the world around you. You seek to possess and control things with the goal being to manipulate energy and how and where it is focused. The results of this change in attitude about self have caused imbalances to manifest in my Plant, Mineral, and Animal Kingdoms. Do you not understand that when you upset the deli-cate balance in any of Nature's Kingdoms and her Elements that all forms of life, including your own, suffer from your actions?

Whenever the Human Kingdom chooses not to take respon-sibility for its effects on other life forms, then Nature and I must step in to reestablish a new balance in the energy fields that operate through my physical body, as well as those that are out-side its exterior. No part of me is totally protected when Nature or I initiate changes in the energy. Some areas of my being will experience these changes in a more dramatic way than others. Know, however, that all life forms will experience the effects of our actions.

Keep in mind that change is inevitable in all things. What I am referring to is the quality and intensity of the actual process of change. Shifts in the landmasses are not to be feared. They are a natural process of the perfection and spiritual growth of my being. What you think and feel about changes occurring in any land mass can determine whether you experience this process in some painful manner or whether you go through it with me, feeling and knowing that perfection and healing are taking place within you as well.

It is true that members of the Mineral, Plant, and Animal Kingdoms can balance all imbalances that you experience within the Human Kingdom.

You can ensure that my physical body is healthy and supportive of all life forms, including generations of your offspring. There have always been sufficient energy resources available to meet the needs of all forms of life. You are encouraged to be creative in seeking alternative means of satisfying your energy needs. When you give up your self-centeredness towards life itself, then ways of working with energy in a more healthy way will be revealed to you.

When you speak of planetary peace, know, my beloved lifestreams, that this can only be when each of you knows the presence of Unconditional Love within the heart. All the imbalanced emotional energies, such as hate, anger, jealousy, and greed, can be released so that you experience peace. Love yourself so that your love can then extend to all other forms of life and to Me.

ENDNOTES

Chapter 1

1. Wallace G. Richardson and Lenora Huett, *The Spiritual Value of Gemstones* (Marina del Rey, CA: DeVorss & Co., 1980), pp. 16-18.

Chapter 3

1. Bernard Gunther, *Energy Ecstasy and Your Seven Vital Chakras* (North Hollywood, CA: Newcastle Publishing Co., 1983), p. 78.

Chapter 7

1. John Diamond, M.D., *Life Energy: Unlocking the Hidden Power of Your Emotions to Achieve Total Well-Being.* (New York: Dodd, Mead & Co., 1985), p. 18.

BIBLIOGRAPHY

Anderson, B. W. *Gemstones for Everyman*. New York: Van Nostrand Reinhold Co., 1976.

Arem, Joel E. *Color Encyclopedia of Gemstones*. New York: Van Nostrand Reinhold Co., 1978.

The Audubon Society Field Guide to North American Rocks and Minerals. New York: Alfred A. Knopf, Inc., 1978.

David, William. *The Harmonics of Sound, Color, and Vibration*. Marina del Rey, Calif.: DeVorss & Co., 1980.

Desautels, Paul E. *The Gem Collection*. Washington, D.C.: Smithsonian Institution Press, 1979.

Diamond, John, M.D. *Life Energy: Unlocking the Hidden Power of Your Emotions to Achieve Total Well-Being*. New York: Dodd, Mead $ Co., 1985.

Gerber, Richard. M.D. *Vibrational Medicine*. Santa Fe, NM.: Bear & Co., 1988.

Gunther, Bernard. *Energy, Ecstasy, and Your Seven Vital Chakras*. North Hollywood, Calif.: Newcastle Publishing Co., 1983.

Isaacs, Thelma. *Gemstones, Crystals, and Healing*. Black Mountain, NC: Lorien house, 1982.

Keyes, Laurel Elizabeth. *Toning: The Creative Power of the Voice*. Marina del Rey, Calif.: DeVorss & Co., 1980.

Richardson, Wallace G., and Lenora Huett. *The Spirtual Value of Gemstones*. Marina del Rey, Calif.: DeVorss & Co., 1980.

Sabetti, Stephano. *The Wholeness Principle*. Sherman Oaks, Calif.: Life Energy Media, 1986.

Schumann, Walter. *Gemstones of the World.* New York: Sterling Publishing Co., Inc. 1977.

Sun Bear and Wabun. *The Medicine Wheel—Earth Astrology.* New York: Prentice-Hall, 1980.

INDEX

A

Absorption spectrum, 27
Affinities, chakra and subtle body, 61, 62
Affirmation, 76
    Gemstone, 213-219
Agate, 31
    Fire, 31, 205
    Moss, 208
Air, 104, 111, 115, 119, 121, 131, 133, 143,
    145, 161, 162, 163, 173, 174, 182, 183,
    185, 187, 74, 84, 124
Alexaderite, 77, 213
    cocreating with, 78
    physical aspects of, 77
    spiritual aspects of, 78
Affirmation, 78, 213
Amazonite, 79, 210, 213
    affinities, 80
    affirmation, 80, 213
    cocreating with, 80
    Deva, 79
    physical aspects, 79
    spiritual aspect, 79

Amber, 81, 207, 208, 213
    affirmation, 82, 213
    cocreating with, 82
    Deva, 81
    physical aspects, 81
    spiritual aspects, 81
Amethyst, 30, 82, 206, 213
    affirmation, 83, 213
    Deva, 82
    physical aspects of, 82
    spiritual aspects, 82
    cocreating with, 83
Apatite, 83, 213
    affirmation, 85, 213
    cocreating with, 85
    Deva, 84
Aquamarine, 85, 209, 213
    affirmation, 86, 213
    cocreating with, 86
    Deva, 85
    physical aspects, 85
Attitudes, positive mental, 35
Aura, 33
Aventurine, 86, 213, 207, 208, 209
    affirmation, 87, 213

cocreating with, 87
Deva, 87
physical aspects, 86
spiritual aspects, 87
Azurite, 88, 206, 213
   affirmation, 89, 213
   chakra affinities, 88
   cocreating with, 89
   Deva, 88
   physical aspects, 88
   spiritual aspects, 88

B

Black tourmalinated quartz, 30
Base of Spine, 153
Beliefs, the influence of, 41
Beryl, 32
   aquamarine, 32
   emerald, 32
Bloodstone, 89, 205, 213
   affirmation, 90, 213
   cocreating with, 90
   Deva, 89
   physical aspects, 89
   spiritual aspects, 90
Blue Lace Agate, 31, 90, 209, 213
   affirmation, 91, 213
   cocreating with, 91
   Deva, 91
   physical aspects, 90
   spiritual aspects, 91
Blue, 55
Body, emotional, 34
   mental, 34
   spiritual subtle, 34
Brilliant cut, 28

C

Cabochon, 28, 43
Calcite, 92, 213
   cocreating with blue, 94

physical aspects, 92
spiritual aspects, 92
Blue, 205
   affirmation, 94, 214
   Deva, 93
   spiritual aspects 93
   green 205
   affirmation, 93, 213
   cocreating with, 93
   Deva, 92
   Honey, 205, 208
Carnelian, 94
   Carnelian, physical aspects, 94
   Orange, 207, 208
     affirmation, 95, 214
     cocreating with, 95
     Deva, 95
     spiritual aspects, 95
   Yellow, 207, 208
     affirmation, 96, 214
     Deva, 96
     spiritual aspects, 96
Celestites 96, 205, 206, 214
   affirmation, 97, 214
   cocreating with, 97
   Deva, 97
   physical aspects, 96
   spiritual aspects, 97
Chakra, 35, 64
   affinties, 78
   crown, 57, 65
   lower abdomen, 57, 65
   root, 57, 65
   solar plexus, 57, 65
   third eye, 57, 65
   throat, 57, 65
Chalcedony, 98, 205, 214
   affirmation, 99, 214
   cocreating, 98
   Deva, 98
   physical aspects, 98
   spiritual aspects, 98

Charoite, 99, 214
    affirmation, 100, 214
    cocreating with, 100
    Deva, 99
    physical aspects of, 99
    spiritual aspects, 100
Chemical compositions, 23
Christ, 69
Chrysoberyl, 77
Chrysocolla, 100, 205, 214
    affirmation, 102, 214
    cocreating with, 101
    Deva, 101
    physical aspects, 100
    spiritual aspects, 101
Chrysoprase, 102, 207, 208, 214
    affirmation, 103, 214
    cocreating with, 103
    Deva, 102
    physical aspects, 102
Citrine, 30, 103, 208, 210, 214
    affirmation, 104, 214
    cocreating with, 104
    Deva, 103-104
    physical aspects, 103
    spiritual aspects, 104
Clear quartz crystal, 22, 62
Clear quartz, 30
Clearing, 205, 206
Cleavage, 27
Clients, Gem essence for, 211-212
Cocreating, for healing, 193
Color, 25, 54
    meditations, 57
    opaque, 25
    translucent 25
    transparent, 25
    developing a sense of, 56-57
Compassion, 69, 70
Conclusion, 232
Consciousness, 41, 75
Copper, 188, 205, 219
    affirmation, 189, 219

    cocreating with, 189
    Deva, 188
    physical aspects, 188
    spiritual aspects, 189
Coral, 104
    physical aspects, 104-105
    Red, 205
        affirmation, 107, 214
        cocreating with, 106
        Deva, 106
        spiritual aspects, 106
    White, 205
        affirmation, 106, 214
        cocreating with, 106
        Deva, 105
        spiritual aspects, 105
Core of balance, 72
Corundum, 32
    Ruby, 32
    Sapphire, 32
Crown, 124, 131, 133, 143, 161, 163, 168,
    190, 191, 206, 228, 229, 230
Crystaline formations, 24
    cubic system, 24
    hexagonal system, 24
    orthorhombic system, 24
    tetragonal system, 24
Crystalline Structure, 23
Cutting and polishing, 28
Cutting, lapidary work, 28

D

Deposits, types of, 29
Deva, 37, 38, 40, 60, 75
    clear crystal quartz, 37
    Overlighting, 38, 233, 236
    the Alexaderite, 78
Devic
    channeling, 75, 76
    Kingdom, 39
    Kingdoms, the spirituality of, 37

Diamond, 107, 210, 214
    affirmation, 109, 214
    cocreating with, 108
    Deva, 107-108
    physical aspects, 107
    spiritual aspects, 108
Dioptase, 109, 215
    affirmation, 110, 215
    cocreating with, 110
    Deva, 109
    physicl aspects, 109
    spiritual aspects, 109
Divine
    Essence, 82
    Divine Sources, 37
    Divine Will, 38

E

Earth, 74, 90, 91, 95, 102, 112, 116, 118,
    122, 135, 156, 171, 179, 182, 187
    element, 74
    energy, 33
    plane, 74
Element, 51
Emerald, 110, 209, 210, 215
    affirmation, 111, 215
    cocreating with, 111
    Deva, 110-111
    physical aspects, 110
    spiritual aspects, 111
    step cut, 28
    emotions and beliefs, clear
        negative, 68
Energy, 33
    earth, 33
    Life-force, 34
        electromagnetic properties of, 36
    movements of, 73
Etheric body, 34
Eye, 206

F

Facet, 28
Feldspar, 31
    Amoazonite, 31
    Labradorite, 31
    Moonstone, 31
Feldspar,
    Orange, 31
    Yellow orthoclase, 32
    Yellow, 207, 208
Fire Agate, 112, 215
    affirmation, 113, 215
    cocreating with, 112
    Deva, 112
    physical aspects, 112
    spiritual aspects, 112
Fire, 74, 90, 112, 126, 129, 130, 135, 137,
    147, 148, 152, 153, 155, 158, 160, 161,
    162, 167, 171, 185, 189, 190,
Fluorite, 113
    physical aspects, 113
    Clear, 206
        affirmation, 114, 215
        cocreating with, 114
        Deva, 113
        spiritual aspects, 114
    Purple, 210
        affirmation, 115, 215
        cocreating with, 115
        Deva, 114
        spiritual aspects, 115
Frequency band, 71
Friedrich Mohs 22

G

Galena, 76, 116, 206
    affirmation, 117, 215
    cocreating with, 117
    Deva, 116
    physical aspects, 116
    spiritual aspects, 116

Garnet, 117, 207, 215
  affirmation, 118, 215
  cocreating with, 118
  Deva, 118
  physical aspects, 117
  spiritual aspects, 118
Gem
  elixirs, 197
  energy perspectives, 53
    Sound, 58
  energy, 53
    chakra and subtle body affinities,
      61, 62
    three-step healing process, 67
    the four elements. 67
  essence, 76, 195, 197, 198
    preparation, 195
    taking the, 201-202
    taking the, guidelines, 201-202
    use, 195
  remedies, 197
  Silica, 119, 215
    affirmation, 120, 215
    cocreating with, 119
    Deva, 119
    spiritual aspects, 119
  tincures, 197
  water, 195, 197
Gemstones, 21, 75, 77
  caring for, 44
  and Healing, 221
  correlations, 42
  care of your, 49
  choosing, 49, 53
  and clear quartz crystal, 227-228
  making, mechanical method,
    197-198
  making, the conscious method,
    199-201
  spiritual aspects of, 33
Gold, 189, 207, 208, 209, 210, 219
  affirmation, 190, 219
  cocreating with, 190

Deva, 198-190
  physical aspects, 189
  spiritual aspects, 190
Grad, Dr. Bernard, 196
Green, 55
Grid, 228
  Energy Light, 235
Grounding, 72
Guardian Angel, 69

H

Hardness, Mohs scale of, 23
Heart, 86, 87, 111, 119, 129, 158, 151, 152,
  155, 157, 177, 182, 191, 229, 230
Heliodor, 120, 215
  affirmation, 121, 215
  cocreating with, 121
  Deva, 120
  physical aspects, 120
  spiritual aspects, 121
Hematite, 121, 215
  affirmation, 122, 215
  cocreating with, 122
  Deva, 122
  physical aspects, 121
  spiritual aspects, 122
Higher Consciousness, 221
Higher Self, 40, 47, 196, 200
Higher Will, 200
Highest Spiritual expression, 200
Human Kingdom, 38, 39, 40, 118, 233,
  236, 234, 235, 237

I

Igneous, 29
Imitation, 28
Impurities, 26
Inclusions, 26
Indigo, 56
Intuitive guidance, asking for, 46

Iolite, 123, 210, 215
  affirmation, 124, 215
  cocreating with, 124
  Deva, 123
  physical aspects, 123
  spiritual aspects, 124

J

Jade, 124, 215, 205, 206, 208, 209, 210
  affirmation, 125, 215
  cocreating with, 125
  Nephrite, Deva, 125
  physical aspects, 124
  spiritual aspects, 125
Jasper, 125, 215
  affirmation, 127, 215
  cocreating with, 126
  Deva, 126
  physical aspects, 125-126
  spiritual aspects, 126
Jet, 127, 215
  affirmation, 128, 215
  cocreating with, 128
  Deva, 127
  physical aspects, 127
  spiritual aspects, 127

K

Kabbalah, 43
Kingdoms of Nature, 18, 36, 38, 39, 41,
  67, 69, 70, 72
Kunzite, 128
  physical aspects, 128
  Clear, 210
    affirmation, 130, 216
    cocreating with, 130
    Deva, 130
    spiritual aspects, 130
    Lavender-pink, 209
    affirmation, 130, 215

  coreating with, 129
  Deva, 128-129
  spiritual aspects, 129
Kyanite, 131, 210, 216
  affirmation, 132, 216
  cocreating with, 132
  Deva, 131
  physical aspects, 131
  spiritual aspects, 131

L

Labradorite, 132, 210, 216
  affirmation, 134, 216
  cocreating with, 134
  Deva, 132-133
  physical aspects, 132
  spiritual aspects, 133
Lapidaries, 44
Lapis Lazuli, 134, 206, 210, 216
  affirmation, 135, 216
  cocreating with, 135
  Deva, 134-135
  physical aspects, 134
  spiritual aspects, 135
Larimar, 135, 209, 216
  affirmation, 137, 216
  cocreating with, 137
  Deva, 136
  physical aspects, 135
  spirtual aspects, 136
Layouts, choosing and working
  with, 226
  Three Criteria for, 224-225
Lepidolite, 137, 216
  affirmation, 138, 216
  cocreating with, 138
  Deva, 137-138
  physical aspects, 137
  spiritual aspects, 138
Life, Oneness of All, 35
Life-force energy levels, 68
Light, Unconditional, 71

Love, Unconditional, 69, 71, 233, 236, 237
Lower abdomen, 102, 112, 122, 126, 147, 156, 164, 170, 171, 176, 177, 186, 191, 207, 229, 230, 87, 90, 95

M

Magic Markers, 57
Magnetite, 138, 205, 207, 216
   affirmation, 139, 216
   cocreating, 139
   Deva, 139
   physical aspects, 138
   spiritual aspects, 139
Malachite, 60, 139, 205, 216
   affirmation, 140, 216
   cocreating with, 140
   Deva, 140
   physical aspects, 139-140
   spiritual aspects, 140
Metals, The, 188
Metamorphic, 29, 30
Mineral, 21
   Families, 30
   Kingdom, 17, 22, 39, 46, 69, 75, 233, 234, 235, 237, 249
Mining, types of, 29
Mixed cut, 28
Moldavite, 141, 210, 216
   affirmation, 143, 216
   cocreating with, 143
   physical aspects, 141-142
   spiritual aspects, 143
Moonstone, 143, 205, 206, 210, 216
   affirmation, 144, 216
   cocreating with, 144
   Deva, 143-144
   physical aspects, 143
   spiritual aspects, 144
Moss Agate, 145, 216
   affirmation, 146, 216
   cocreating with, 146

Deva, 145
   physical aspects, 145
   spiritual aspects, 145
Mountains, Ural, 77

N

Nature 18, 42
   elements of, 72
   four elements of, 19
   tones, 60

O

Obsidian, 146, 205, 216
   affirmation, 148, 216
   cocreating with,
   Deva, 146-147
   physical aspects, 146
   spiritual aspects, 147
Opal, 148, 206, 210, 216
   affirmation, 148, 216
   cocreating with, 148
   Deva, 148
   physical aspects, 148
   spiritual aspects, 148
Orange, 54
Orthorhombic system, 77

P

Pearl, 150, 216, 205, 206
   affirmation, 151, 216
   cocreating with, 151
   Deva, 150-151
   physical aspects, 150
   spiritual aspects, 151
Pegmatites, 29
Pendulum charts, 203-210
Pendulum, crystal, 47
   Questions to ask your crystal, 49

Peridot, 151, 208, 209, 217
    affirmation, 152, 217
    cocreating with, 152
    Deva, 152
    physical aspects, 151-152
    spiritual aspects, 152
Physical aspects, 25, 75, 77, 119
Pink, 56
Plain cut, 28
Planetary Overview, 233-237
Pleochroism, 26
Pranayama, 73
process, infusing or building, 70
Pyrite, 76, 153, 207, 217
    affirmation, 154, 217
    cocreating with, 153
    Deva, 153
    physical aspects, 153
    spiritual aspects, 153

Q

Quartz, 30, 60
    Black tourmalinated, 207, 208, 209
        affirmation, 179, 218
        cocreating with, 179
        Deva, 179
        physical aspects, 179
        spiritual aspects, 179
    Clear, 206, 207, 208, 209
    Microcrystalline, 30, 31
        Aventurine, 31
        Bloodstone, 31
        Carnelian, 31
        Chalcedony, 31
        Chrysoprase, 31
        Heliotrope, 31
        Moss agate, 31
        Tiger's eye, 31
    Rose, 209
    rutilated, 205, 206
    Smokey, 208
quick cleaning, 44

R

Receiving hand, 36
Reconstructed, 28
Red, 54
Refractive index, 27
Rhodochrosite, 154, 205, 217
    affirmation, 155, 217
    cocreating with, 155
    Deva, 154
    physical aspects, 154
    spiritual aspects, 155
Rhodonite, 155, 205, 217
    affirmation, 156, 217
    cocreating with, 156
    Deva, 155-156
    physical aspects, 155
    spiritual aspects, 156
Rock, 21
    formations, three types , 29
Root, 90, 112, 118, 122, 126, 139, 153, 158,
    164, 170, 171, 179, 184, 190, 191, 207,
    229, 230
Rose Quartz, 30, 156, 217
    affirmation, 157, 217
    cocreating with, 157
    Deva, 157
    physical aspects, 156
    spiritual aspects, 157
Ruby, 157, 207, 209, 217
    affirmation, 159, 217
    cocreating with, 158
    Deva, 158
    physical aspects, 157-158
    spiritual aspects, 158
Rutilated Quartz, 30, 76, 159, 217
    affirmation, 160, 217
    cocreating with, 160
    Deva, 159
    physical aspects, 159
    spiritual aspects, 160
Ryerson, Kevin, 196

S

Sapphire, 160
    physical aspects, 160-161
    Blue, 206, 210
        affirmation, 162, 217
        cocreating with, 162
        Deva, 162
        spiritual aspects, 162
    clear, 206, 210
        affirmation, 162, 217
        cocreating with, 161
        Deva, 161
        spiritual aspects, 161
Saturation, 51
Sedimentary, 29
Selenite, 162, 210
    affirmation, 164, 217
    cocreating with, 164
    Deva, 163
    physical aspects, 162-163
    spiritual aspects, 163
self-acceptance, 70
Sending hand, 36
Sensing hand, 36
Silicon dioxide, 30
Silver, 190, 205, 206, 219
    affirmation, 191, 219
    cocreating with, 191
    Deva, 191
    physical aspects, 190
    spiritual aspects, 191
Smoky Quartz, 30, 164, 217
    affirmation, 165, 217
    cocreating with, 165
    Deva, 164
    physical aspects, 164
    spiritual aspects, 164
Sodalite, 165, 210, 217
    affirmation, 166, 217
    cocreating with, 166
    Deva, 165
    physical aspects, 165
    spiritual aspects, 166
Solar plexus, 84, 87, 90, 95, 102, 104, 122, 144, 145, 147, 152, 155, 156, 164, 167, 171, 173, 176, 177, 184, 186, 190, 208, 229, 230, 231
Soul tone, 52, 59, 60
Soul tones, Gemstone, 213-219
Specific gravity, 27
Spinel, Red, 166, 205, 217
    affirmarion, 168, 217
    cocreating with, 167
    Deva, 167
    physical aspects, 166
    spiritual aspects, 167
Spiritual
    aspects, 75
    consciousness, 51, 234
    dimensions, 36
    expansion, 71
    forms, 36
    levels of reality, 33
    expansion, 207, 208, 209, 210
stone, 21
    Deva, 200
    hardess 22
    working with one or two, 225-226
Sugilite, 168, 206, 210, 217
    affirmation, 169, 217
    cocreating with, 169
    Deva, 168
    physical aspects, 168
    spiritual aspects, 168
Sun, Deva, 200
Sunstone, orange, 169, 207, 218
    affirmation, 170, 218
    cocreating with, 170
    Deva, 169-170
    physical aspects, 169
    spiritual aspects, 170
Sythetic genstones, 29

T

Table facet, 28
Third eye, 88, 104, 111, 115, 119, 121,
     124, 130, 131, 133, 135, 143, 144, 148,
     151, 161, 162, 163, 168, 173, 174, 183,
     187, 191, 221, 228, 229, 230, 231
Throat, 119, 136, 190, 205, 229, 230, 86,
     91
Thymus Gland, 35, 143, 145, 182, 189,
     190, 222-224, 229, 230
     strength test, 222-223
Tiger's eye, 170, 207, 208, 218
     affirmation, 171, 218
     cocreating, 171
     Deva, 171
     physical aspects, 170
     spiritual aspects, 171
Tones, 59
Toning, 58
Topaz, 171
     Topaz, physical aspects, 171-172
     Blue, 210
         affirmation, 174, 218
         cocreating with, 174
         Deva, 174
         spiritual aspects, 174
     Clear, chakra affinities, 172
         cocreating with, 172
         Deva, 172
         spiritual aspects, 172
     Yellow, 208, 210
         affirmation, 174, 218
         cocreating with, 173
         Deva, 173
         spiritual aspects, 173
Tourmaline, 175
     Black, 179
     Blue, 208, 209, 210
         affirmation, 180, 218
         cocreating with, 180
         physical aspects, 180
         spiritual aspects, 180

Green, 207, 209
     affirmation, 176, 218
     cocreating with, 176
     Deva, 175
     physical aspects, 175
     spiritual aspects, 176
Pink, 207, 208, 209
     affirmation, 177, 218
     cocreating with, 177
     Deva, 177
     physical aspects, 177
Watermelon, 207, 208, 209
     affirmation, 178, 218
     cocreating with, 178
     Deva, 178
     physical aspects, 178
     spiritual aspects, 178
Turquoise, 60, 181, 209, 219
     affirmation, 182, 219
     cocreating with, 182
     Deva, 181
     physical aspects, 181
     spiritual aspects, 182

U

Ulexite, 182, 219
     affirmation, 183, 219
     cocreating with, 183
     Deva, 182-183
     physical aspects, 182
     spiritual aspects, 183
Universal Oneness, 39

V

Vanadinite, 184, 219
     affirmation, 185, 219
     cocreating, 185
     Deva, 184
     physical aspects, 184
     spiritual aspects, 184
Violet, 56

W

Water, 74, 86, 87, 119, 122, 129, 130, 139,
      144, 151, 155, 156, 157, 164, 168,
      170, 176, 177, 186, 191, 196
   as a medium, 196
   Deva, 200

Y

Yellow Orthoclase Feldspar, 185, 219
   affirmation, 186, 219
   cocreating with, 186
   Deva, 185-186
   physical aspects, 185
   spiritual aspects, 186
Yellow, 55

Z

Zireon, 186, 219
   affirmation, 188, 219
   cocreating with, 187-188
   Deva, 187
   physical aspects, 186-187
   spiritual aspects, 187
Zodiac, 42, 43

ABOUT THE AUTHORS

P amela L. Chase MS and Jonathan Pawlik have been working with the Mineral Kingdom as healers and counselors for more than 15 years, and crystals and gemstones have played a key role in their own healing journey. They are also the co-authors of *Healing with Crystals* and *Trees for Healing*.